SAN LUIS OBISPO COUNTY CALIFORNIA HISTORY

1542-1917

by

Benjamin Brooks

A 2020 Reprint
by
Kenneth E. Bingham

**San Luis Obispo County California History
1542-1917** *by*
Benjamin Brooks

A 2020 Reprint by Kenneth E. Bingham

Cover Design By Kenneth E. Bingham

From The Original Books:
History Of Santa Barbara, San Luis Obispo and Ventura Counties California By:
C. M. Gidney, Of Santa Barbara County Benjamin Brooks, Of San Luis Obispo
County Edwin M. Sheridan, Of Ventura County
Illustrated Volume I

FOREWORD

As will be noted, portions of this sketch have been contributed by local writers of special competency; the review of the religious interests by Rev. C. H. F. Chandler, Rector of St. Stephen's Episcopal Church of San Luis Obispo ; the later development of educational interests by Mr. A. H. Mahley, superintendent of that city's schools and by Mr. Guy E. Heaton, horticultural commissioner of the county, treating of matters within his special province. Their assistance is gratefully acknowledged by the publishers. For the rest of the work the author is unable to shift the responsibility. It has been his endeavor to invest the story of the county with some degree of human interest, avoiding dry details and personal references. He has followed largely the pictures that hang on memory's wall and as the gallery covers a residence of over sixty years in the state, more than half of which has been spent in this county, the tale is necessarily hurried and imperfect. But such as it is, it is told by one who was frequently an active participant in the events recorded and always a deeply interested observer.

A

1877

9-M.E.
North Church

3-Court House

B

20-Grist Mill

12-Bank

6-Presbyterian Church

13-Gas Works

5-Masonic Hall

19-French Hotel

14-Tribune Office

4-City Hall

15-Water Co. O.

7-M.E South Church

Mission

17-Sacred Heart School

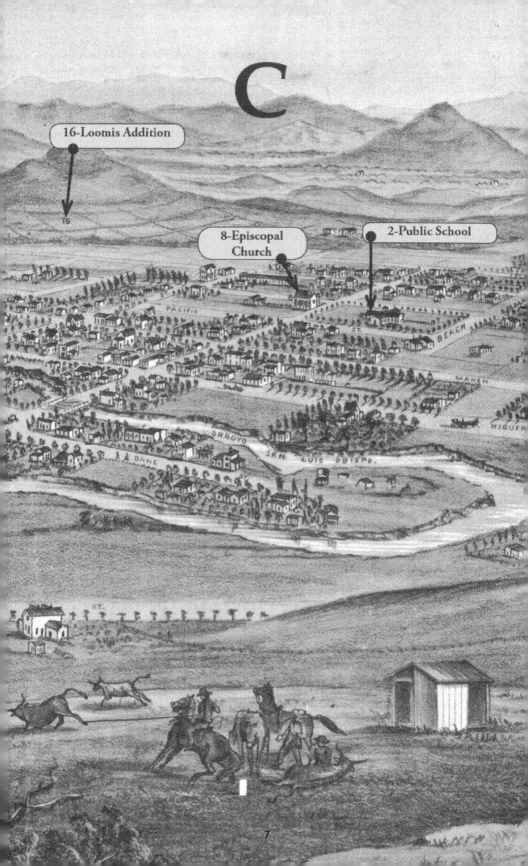

16-Loomis Addition

8-Episcopal Church

2-Public School

D

10-R.R. Depot

SAN LUIS OBISPO COUNTY

CHAPTER I

INTRODUCTORY

History, as commonly apprehended, is largely confined to the wars and bloodshed which have afflicted the unhappy country in question and the glorification of the heroes who have marched to fame over the bodies of their fellowcountrymen. Hence the dictum that the happy land is that which has no history. In which view San Luis Obispo county may be deemed supremely blessed for although repeatedly her nationality has been changed, it has been incidentally only, her soil has never been soaked with the blood of her people and except in the somewhat opera bouffe transactions of the American "conquest," grim-visaged war has never afflicted her. And so in endeavoring to recount the story of the occupation, growth and development of the county, nothing is to be set down but the slender annals of a peaceful and peace-loving people, whose arms were the plowshare and the pruning hook and who looked for conquest only over the forces of Nature, whose benignity offered not a shadow of hostility. Vague and dim myths, miraculously preserved bits of human skull, scratches upon the walls of long-hidden caves, shadowy records of human intelligence, lend credence to the belief that a hundred centuries ago or more, man existed upon the earth but during all those ages his habitat seemed to be confined to a small portion of the eastern hemisphere. Again and again, in repeated palimpsests, he has inscribed the records of his national existence, its beginning, rise, fall and extinction but his theatre of action, has apparently, only in more recent ages, extended to this western continent. The vast expanses of ocean have been unconquerable barriers. This portion of the world's surface has been reserved for the overflow of an over-crowded earth. It is not too much to say that like the wine at the Cana wedding feast, the best has been kept to the last. It is true as to the ripened adaptibility of the continent to man's use; it is more especially true if we regard

1

the ripened humanity itself. Behind all the glamour of past ages, the storied achievements of world conquerors, marvelous monuments of architecture that have defied the tooth of Time, looms the black and bloody background of a world of human beings, enthralled in ignorance and superstitution, dumb bondsmen under despotic rule. Down to more recent days, and it is not to be pretended that the exhibition is yet entirely over, the human procession was eternally the same. A decorated and decorative few the vast mass slowly emerging from the primitive brute. Despite the fact that war was never more colossal than in these latter days, that there are still rulers who dispose at their will of the lives and fortunes of their millions of subjects and that there are still millions who are content to be subjects or who have no option, the fact remains that the masses of mankind have as a whole reached a higher plane of civilization and exhibit an average of intelligence that renders the existence of the historical despot or the desperate degradation of slavish multitudes alike impossible. Wars may never cease and there may always be evil men to foment them but the peoples will not, consciously at least, take up arms to enslave their fellows. The world has moved and it still moves and always toward the light. If it is not the Millenium, it is at least its dawn, with new heavens and a new and virgin earth, free from the gathered corruption of eons of evil passion and with a distinctly improved race of men, for its inhabitants.

PHYSICAL ASPECTS

San Luis Obispo county lies between the 35th and 36th parallels of latitude. It occupies about ninety miles, nearly one-tenth of California's ocean front. Beginning at the mouth of the Santa Maria river, the northern boundary of the neighboring county of Santa Barbara the shore line winds northwesterly to the sixth parallel, the southern limit of Montery county. Viewed from the ocean, during the long rainless summer months, in brilliant sunshine and under cloudless skies, its long stretches of beach, laced and spangled with the slow-reaching waves, its boundary walls of beautifully colored hills, it is a fairy spectacle. But doubtless to the eye of Cabrillo, to whom history credits its first discovery, nearly four centuries ago, as that dauntless mariner clung to the rigging of his curious little cockle-shell of a vessel, on a dark November day, the ocean storm lashed into fury, the mountainous waves thundering upon the shore and dashing in great geysers of surf and spray far up the rocky points it must have seemed a most sinister and menacing lee shore, to be skirted with apprehension and at a safe distance. Today under the same conditions, the skilled seaman guides his bark with all confidence into Port San Luis, where by the expenditure of a few hundreds of thousands of dollars, a breakwater has been constructed, within whose sheltering arm, great deep sea vessels dock with safety. And except when the infrequent gales of winter prevail, smaller vessels make safe landing at Point Buchon, at Cayucos and San Simeon, while the long smooth beaches afford a favorite resort for thousands fleeing from the inclement

San Luis Obispo

heat of the interior valleys of the state. From the Pacific, the county extends eastward to the Coast range, which in its sinuous course, closely parallels the shore line, forming a parallellogram about two-thirds the size of the state of Connecticut, embracing about 3,334 square miles or 3,290,000 acres. From a hovering aeroplane, the general corrugated aspect of the county might suggest doubts as to its agricultural value. The land rises rapidly, even at times precipitately, from the shore line, falling away again towards the interior where it maintains an average altitude of six or eight hundred feet and although there are wide expanses of plain, still the country might be described as chiefly "rolling."

Of keen interest to the geologist has been the long evolution of this section of the earth. Far back in those geological "periods" comparable in extent to "light years" of space, the records of the rocks display California as submerged thousands of feet beneath the ocean which washed the base of the Sierras, scattered islands alone indicating the ultimate expanse of the continent. During the ages, there were oscillations, upheavals and depressions, sometimes catastrophic, sometimes immeasurably slow. At times the loftier elevations along the ultimate coast line, confined in the basins of the interior an island sea of vast extent and doubtless only a gentle depression of the sky line marked the gap of the future Golden Gate. Rivers flowing westward sought the ocean. In the latter days, perhaps immediately previous to the present physical status, the land seemed to have emerged from the depths of ocean by well-defined steps. The evidences of all of which, recognizable even by the layman, are the ancient river beds, trending westward, the still extensive deposits of huge marine shells yet in place on some of the highest elevations of the county, 2,000 feet above sea level and the well-marked terraces, beaches and shore lines, traceable for miles at varying heights. As a minor incident in these tremendous convulsions, the upper strata destined for man's occupation has been curiously rolled up and distorted. Successive chains of mountains, generally parallelling the coast, not always continuous but all spurs of the Coast range, rise at times to a height of 3,000 feet above sea level, the strata of which they are composed dipping in various directions and in varying degrees, sometimes approaching the perpendicular. But in spite of these rugged birth-throes, perhaps because of them, only a small percentage of the great area of the county may be characterized as waste or valueless. In the aeons of time which have passed since this "dry land" assumed its present conformation, the rich and fertile soil evolved by the forces of Nature has filled the deep ravines and wide gorges, transforming them into broad expanses of valley and plateau and have even blanketed the low hills and lesser elevations that tickled with the hoe, smile with abundant harvest. But it is not alone the levelling processes of Nature, of erosion and denudation, by winds and rains and beating suns, transforming the successive ranges of bleak and barren granite into habitable slopes and plains which have made the Eden of today. Even in Alaska may be found vast level expanses of wonderfully fertile land. The beneficent processes of Nature are here perpetual and unceasing. It is a land of "the early and the latter rains." Simple fertility of soil is not its only appeal to its inhabitant. If that alone was final, the preference might well go to the torrid silts of Imperial valley, the irrigated plains of the

4

San Joaquin and other interior valleys, perhaps to the far northern Pacific states. Climatic conditions are the ultimate factor. The westerly winds, practically constant throughout the year, have the uniform temperature of the great ocean over which they sweep and moderate the solar heat which in this latitude at sea level would doubtless be excessive. From the ocean come also the winter storms with their plentiful rainfall. Says Professor C. Abbe of the U. S. Weather Bureau: "The prevailing easterly drift of the atmosphere in temperate latitudes, causing the well-known winds from the west, is one of the prime factors in modifying the climate of the coast of California. This Coast line, stretching from ten degrees of latitude, is subjected to a steady indraft of air from the west. In this movement, together with the fact that to the west is the great Pacific Ocean, lies the secret of the difference in temperature between the Atlantic and the Pacific coasts at places of like latitude." Says Leigh H. Irvine, a distinguished writer: "The rotation of the earth on its axis in the whirl of more than a thousand miles an hour from west to east determines the easterly drift of the winds in the northern hemisphere. The prevailing winds from the west, say at Chicago, bring the breath of winter from fields of snow and ice. In the summer months the same winds from the west, fresh from hot and arid regions, bring sunstroke and melting heat, cyclones and the many rigors of severe seasons. It is different on the Coast because of the origin of the winds, which sweep over thousands of miles of the Pacific whose average temperature is fifty-five degrees above zero, Fahrenheit." The direct and immediate effect of the beneficent westerly winds upon the climate of our county is obvious. At rare intervals during the winter months, the winds may blow from the north and east, straight from the snow-clad summits of the Sierra Nevadas. For the rest of the year the climatic changes are determined by the conflict between the two great factors, the sun and sea. Were the influences of the sun unopposed, this would be a torrid region, perpetually rainless like the coasts of Peru, comparatively a desert. The ocean projects a perpetual shield over the land of moisture laden winds, tempering the excessive heat and maintaining the temperature after the sun has set. Quite distinctive are the effects of this conflict in different parts of the county. Along the shores the ocean breezes have the advantage. The average temperature is lower, the precipitation greater, there are running streams seldom entirely dry, after the fashion of California rivers in summer. It is a land of lush grasses, of dairies and stock-raising, of barley and beans. A

5

few miles inland, at a higher altitude, a rampart of mountain, cutting off the winds from the ocean, there is a marked change which is emphasized at each successive fold in the earth with its higher altitude and its greater protection from the westerly winds until at the easterly edge of the county we have the minimum rainfall and the highest average temperature in the county. How this interesting matter of the creation of a climate is considered from a scientific point of view is concisely told in the following note on the subject from Father Ricard, the celebrated scientist of the University of Santa Clara:

"Climate in the old sense, means *Inclination*, or the slope of the plane of the horizon at any point on the earth's surface. Hence in the mind of the ancients, it was synonymous with latitude.

"Nowadays, besides latitude, climate takes in that particular combination of weather elements which habitually dominate any particular area on the earth's surface.

"Places at very small distances from each other, have very often entirely different climates, as regards temperature, rainfall, winds, electric conditions, etc.

"Coming to the point in question, would say that San Luis Obispo county must be greatly affected as regards climate, first, by its nearness to the Pacific ocean, the waters of which being always comparitively warm, permit you to bathe almost continuously in an evaporated ocean of genial and balmy air, and, as atmospheric circulation is on the whole from east to west, you cannot be affected as the more eastern counties are, by atmospheric conditions which have been tainted by contact or friction with large tracts of mountainous or level land.

"This makes all the difference in the world between the climates say of San Francisco and New York and again between the climates of valleys near the immediate coast range and the farther inland valleys of the Sacramento and the San Joaquin. Why even such small differences as one, two or three miles can and do make very appreciable and, as the case may be, even enormous differences.

"Secondly, by the lay of the mountains round about and the many gulches that centuries of erosion and denudation have dug here and there along the penchants. Currents of air in opposite directions alternately ply through these gulches. Mountains in the close vicinity of large bodies of water give rise to perpetual sea and land breezes, the former making it feel cool during the hottest days of summer and the latter making a comfortable sleep possible and chasing away the intolerable mosquito.

6

"The mountains of San Luis Obispo county do, moreover, shelter it against the northern blasts of winter and translate their violence into gentleness. On the other hand, the south and southeast winds, being the forerunners or companions of northwestern storms, carry on their wings, stores of moderate temperatures.

"Another great advantage of a topography like that of San Luis Obispo is that barring exceptionally dry winters, the supply of rain must needs be more plentiful than elsewhere. For as we ascend eastward from the sea level, the rainfall is nearly proportionate to the amount in feet of the ascent and this for a couple of reasons that recommend themselves to the meteorological mind.

"(a) The higher we go into the region of air with our feet still resting on the ground, the less its compression and the easier the condensation and fall of water vapor.

"(b) A second reason which explains the first is that the negative ions which carry the steam up from the ocean surface by uniting with the positive electrons of the upper air get rid of their steam content and the latter being left without support, falls to earth straightway. Whereas, away low down in the plains, the opposite reason obtains, the air is hard compressed, condensation and rainfall more difficult and parsimonious.

"The negatively charged earth being further away, its repellant force is correspondingly less. Hence the impact of the negatively charged steam particles with the positively charged upper air, is more subdued and the disengagement of water drops must be proportionately less. Hence it is that in regard to rainfall, mountainous districts are always more favored than the bottoms of the valleys.

"This may easily account for the fact that the county seat of San Luis Obispo county has, every once in a while, a much larger rainfall record than most other places, North or South, East or West."

To some degree, climate is a measurable thing and for the past forty years at least, volunteer physicists or the appointed observers of the U. S. Weather Bureau have accurately noted the rain-fall, the range of the thermometer, and the direction and force of the winds and from their observations it appears that the average climatic conditions maintained at the city of San Luis Obispo are practically identical with those of Mentone, Nice, Mexico and other places considered ideal in that respect; that it is practically constant, that of the 365 days of the year about two-thirds will be radiantly cloudless and perhaps fifty on which any rain falls; that the range of temperature for any given month is repeated with no material variance year after year, and yet being controlled by the impulse of that most inconsistent element, the wind, within its appointed range and to its utmost extent, change is incessant. But after all, while the scientific record will furnish the exact condition of the weather, to be really informed and acquainted with the climate, one must, as John Burroughs says, "consult your senses. The body will tell you what the instrument will not, the character of the day, its balminess, softness, sweetness. The body and mind sympathise with surrounding conditions, implements of precision will not." They cannot tell of the magic that swiftly, seemingly in a few hours, after the first bountiful showers of the early fall, transforms the whole landscape, a brilliant mantle of living green, spreading to the mountain tops and replacing the soft browns and magentas and amethystine hues, painted by the sun during the long rainless summer months. Better than tabulated records of the accomplishments of the elements is the consultation of the senses of a writer and scholar like the late William H. Mills, who said: "Under our summer suns the fruits ripen, unaccompanied by the discomforts of the torrid zone. Here the brown of our summer hills and the golden stubble of the after-harvest are the only winter that we know. Here a spring-like verdure is the harbiger of coming autumn, and autumn is attended by no forewarning of the rigors of winter. Here winter is the season when the warm brown earth is turned by the plow for seed-time, and early spring, with its flowers and ripening grain, is opulent with the prophecy of hopeful industry."

In fine, this last bit of the earth's surface to be subjected to man's dominion is wonderfully interesting. It is a curious problem to the geologist and a fascinating study to the historian.

CHAPTER II

FIRST FOOTPRINTS

There is not anywhere upon the globe a large tract of country, which we have discovered destitute of inhabitants, or whose first population can be fixed with any degree of historical certainty. Gibbon might have had this section of the world in mind when he so philosophised. When the white men first beheld it, it swarmed with human beings. A century and a half passed before it was again visited by the Europeans and in that long interval, the teeming population had apparently greatly diminished. Doubtless, as in New England, shortly before the landing of the Pilgrims or as has been seen in Alaska, some pestilence beyond their power to combat had swept them away. But otherwise the curious explorers found no change in the condition of the natives. Their tales repeat the story of a race hardly developed from the stone age. The aborigines had fire but their implements, the first mark of evolution, were only the bow, the flint-headed arrow and spear, the stone mortar, simple tools for hunting and fishing but no trace of the use of metals except for glittering ornament. Clothes were not needed nor habitations either except as shelter from the rain or protection from the rare danger of wild beasts. Still these naked, untutored savages, passing their aimless lives in unmeasured content were not hardly dealt with by mother Nature. Their wants were easily supplied. The soil volunteered its crops of seeds and roots and berries. Game was plentiful and sea and streams teemed with fish. Their intelligence was adequately developed for their physical needs and even exhibited in some directions skill and ingenuity which excited the surprise and admiration of their first visitors. Viscaino's diarist wrote that the Indians came out in canoes of cedar and pine, made of planks very well joined and caulked, each one with eight oars. They had willow baskets very well made and water vessels resembling flasks, rattan inside and heavily varnished outside. It would task the skill of the modern boat builder to construct boats of that magnitude, intended for use in the open sea, without the use of nails or metal implements of any kind. The heavy varnishing that is mentioned was doubtless with the native bitumen which is so plentiful a product of the county. And as is claimed to be universally the case with the savages of every clime, they were not without notions of a Creative Being and a future life. They were not idolators nor devil worshippers. However, in the scale of evolution, they did not approach the condition of the natives of Central America, whose wondrous remains, architecturally and otherwise, have profoundly interested the archeologist, nor those of the western South American coast where recent explorations have brought to light the fact that in prehistoric times, certain of the arts, such as weaving had reached a degree of excellence quite equal to that of the far-famed Indias themselves. But as we have said, during those centuries of which we have knowledge, the native races remained absolutely unchanged, and the physical conditions remaining the same, there is certainly no "historic certainty" that for countless centuries before, their successive generations had not passed on in endless procession, as fixed and unaltered as the soil they lived on. Perhaps the first populations were autochthenes, indebted for existence to a separate creative fiat. Or perhaps, as is equally probable, they spread to this land from the South Seas, over that great continent of "Pan," which it is fabled, once bridged the vast Pacific, as did mythical "Atlantis," the wide Atlantic.

But while we may regard the aborigines of the county as a fixed quantity for ages and far down in the scale of humanity, their common life after all did not differ so greatly from that of the average human being of a higher type. The same ambitions may be detected. By instinct or reason, they followed the natural laws, to increase and multiply, to care for their progeny and their dependents and to earn their bread by the sweat of their brows. Their notions of comfort might have been limited, their habitations of the rudest, their food and clothing of the scantiest but doubtless they passed their lives contentedly enough and it is not so unusual to find many in these latter days who cut no greater figure in life.

The story of the discovery and conquest of America has always offered a fascinating field for the historian. The chief labor of recent writers has been to destroy much of the embroidery that fertile imagination had woven about the slender array of demonstrated fact. Every one has, from childhood, been as familiar with the lineaments of Columbus as with those of Lincoln or Napoleon and it is somewhat disturbing to learn that the currently accepted portrait of the great discoverer was purely conventional, that no picture of him taken in his lifetime exists and that not one of the hundreds of his supposed portraits were executed by any painter who had ever seen him. Purely mythical too, is the vision of the dreamer, his brow "sicklied o'er with the pale cast of thought," trudging over the dusty Spanish highway in a last despairing effort to appeal to the liberality of the great queen Isabella. No two of the scores of ancient portraits of Columbus resemble each other in the least but all agree in presenting what was even then merely traditional, a man of commanding presence, of fine intelligence and broad vision but first of all a bluff and sturdy mariner. He had sailed all the known seas, had skirted far down the African coast, had rounded the British Isles, the Ultima Thule of the time and had reached Iceland. The shores of the Mediterranean he had known from boyhood. He was of the type of skilled seaman, with whom the merchants of Venice and Portugal adventured their tall argosies "richly fraught." He needed to be a cosmographer and a collector of charts. What the Northmen knew of sea-craft and distant shores and they had ventured far, Columbus had learned from them. To him the earth was a sphere and he could approximate its circumference. He voyaged intelligently over the western sea towards the Indies because the hostile Saracens had ended the rich trade eastward to that goal. And he had to seek financial aid from the despotic rulers of the time because to private capital his daring projects were not alluring from a business standpoint. Nor would it seem after all that he was so inadequately rewarded. To him alone is given the honor and glory of his great enterprise and his name will endure unsullied and illustrious while the hordes of lesser men that trailed after him and gathered in the spoil may have gained riches but are remembered chiefly for their deeds of evil.

During the half century which followed the landing of Columbus, the armed hosts of Spain quite thoroughly explored the vast new territory which that nation had so wonderfully acquired. Cortez had overrun and conquered Mexico; Vaca had traversed the continent from Florida to the Gulf of California; Ulloa, Mendoza and Ximines had traced the shores of that Gulf and skirted those of the peninsula of Lower California; Alarcon had sailed up the Colorado river; Coronado had reached the plains of Kansas. Gold and silver and precious stones had been the lure that led these valiant adventurers on such long and toilsome pilgrimages, encountering many different Indian tribes and suffering incredible hardships but in their search for riches they met only bitter disappointment. The only result of value reached was the demonstration of the vast extent of the new world, the tracing of its east

11

and west coast lines from Florida around the Gulf of Mexico to the isthmus and from Peru to San Diego. It was in 1542 that these long-continued efforts of the treasure hunters were finally directed to the northwestern coast of the continent. Mendoza was then Viceroy of Mexico and it was under his orders that the Portuguese, Juan Rodriguez Cabrillo and his lieutenant Ferrolo, with two small vessels, the San Salvador and the Vitoria, sailed along the coast from Navidad to the 42nd degree of latitude, establishing for Spain, by right of their discoveries, dominion over all that part of the continent of North America. It was a magnificent conquest but from the view-point of Mendoza, a barren one. There was no vast wealth discovered. Ferrolo barely succeeded in regaining his port of departure. Cabrillo, even less fortunate, had met death while wintering at the island of San Miguel. As an incident of the voyage, of capital importance to this county, it is recorded that Cabrillo landed on its shores and it is even claimed was buried here instead of the island of San Miguel. The era of Spanish exploration of these seas practically ceased with the voyage of Cabrillo for nearly sixty years. But long before that the fond dream of Columbus of a new pathway for European commerce to the Indias had been realized. Shortly after the discoveries of Columbus, Magellan had rounded the Cape of Good Hope and pushing on, had discovered the Philippines. In a few years, those islands became the shipping point for a great commerce and the course of the vessels sailing thence eastward, carried them along the California coast from Mendocino to Acapulco. It was in the hope of finding harbors of refuge for the vessels embarked in this trade that in 1602, the Conde de Monterey finally commissioned Sebastian Viscaino, to sail with his ships for the discovery "of harbors and bays of the coast of the South Sea as far as Cape Mendocino." In December of that year Viscaino landed on the shores of the Bay of San Luis Obispo. We were again discovered. But 167 years were still to pass before any attempt at occupation or colonization was to be made. It was only in 1769, after the political destinies of the rest of the North American continent had been practically settled, that Spain, recognizing that to hold the vast territory she claimed in Alta California, actual possession had become necessary, organized expeditions for that purpose. They were confided to the direction of Father Junipero Serra and Gaspar de Portola, names ever illustrious in the history of the state. The political object, that of peopling the country was largely to be attained through the conversion and civilization of the natives. For this purpose, Missions were to be established at short distances from each other as centres of influence and a slender military force at each, lent its assistance and protection to the padres. The objects of the expeditions were very successfully attained and many Missions were established. Among them, on September 1st, 1772, Father Serra founded that of San Luis Obispo de Tolosa.

The attendant ceremonies were of the simplest. The great padre, journeying from Monterey to San Diego, had reached here some days before. He was accompanied by the Commandante Fages, and, as guard, a corporal and four soldiers and on the way he had taken

OLD MISSION, SAN LUIS OBISPO

from the Mission of San Antonio, Fray Jose Caballar, who was to be left in charge of the new institution. They had followed along the coast trail and through the Osos valley and had evidently spent some time in examining the country, and finally with the same unerring judgment exhibited in the location of all the Californian Missions, the site for the new home for the church was determined. It was on a low hill, skirted by perennial streams of water and sheltered by two neighboring peaks, one of which, in some aspects of its rugged sum it exhibited a triple peak and from fanciful association with the dignity of the patron saint of the new foundation, suggested the form of a mitre and received the name of the Bishop's Peak. On this site a rude hut of boughs and brush was made, within it was the altar and on the bough of a nearby sycamore

13

was suspended a bell. At the appointed hour, the ringing of the bell called together the natives, who had gathered in great numbers at the advent of the strangers. Then the priests in their robes performed the dedicatory ceremonies, the erection and adoration of the Cross, the installation of the missionary in charge, the service of the mass, the delivery of the discourse, etc. The Mission duly established, Father Serra and the Commandante on the following day continued their journey southward, leaving with Fray Caballar, the small guard of soldiers, a scanty supply of provisions and a few pounds of sugar with which to trade with the Indians for further supplies. And it is written by Palou of Serra, that with this small outfit, Caballar was "very well contented." He had to be. But after all the outlook was not so desperate. True he was in the far interior of an unknown and newly discovered country, surrounded by hordes of savages of questionable disposition and with whom he could communicate only by signs and completely isolated from other human companionship or help should danger threaten. But on the other hand, his immediate wants were easily supplied and the future held infinite promise. The priest was in sole possession of a kingly territory. He was monarch of all he might have surveyed, even from the top of a high mountain. Several millions of acres were under his dominion, the greater part of which was fertile valley and rolling hill, virgin soil, green with lush growth under the rains and golden with ripened alfileria and waving in- •
digenous grain through the months of sunshine. From the stiff clay, tiles for roofing could be burnt or sun-dried "adobes," even in unskilled hands could be swiftly constructed and piled readily into walls for substantial buildings. From Mexico and Spain could be brought, besides the 21 bulls, 9 cows and 8 calves, the royal endowment at each Mission, tools, implements and machinery and seeds, plants and young trees for fields, vineyards and orchards. With this vast domain at his disposal, with no charges to meet, with an unlimited supply of labor costing nothing what boundless wealth might not be speedily acquired. It was an entrancing vision, swiftly and wonderfully realized. The Franciscan fathers were doubtless sincerely devoted to their main calling, the conversion of the heathen but the material interests of the church were by no means overlooked. As we mentioned, they were at no expense for labor. The natives were tractable and their theological training was suited to their limited intelligence. But their adoption into the bosom of the Church was no idle form. It practically constituted for them a servitude, patriarchal and usually kindly but nevertheless despotic

14

and when exercised by an unkindly priest or a vicious and ferocious soldier might be galling and provocative of rebellion. It provided for their necessities and largely bettered their conditions but it involved a continuous industry which was greatly to the advantage of their benefactors. The labor cost was their subsistence which was simple and economical and caused no material subtraction from the fruits of their labor. And it is of record that in its palmy days, San Luis Obispo was one of the wealthiest of the Californian Missions. At one time it owned "some 80,000 head of cattle, 70,000 sheep, 6,000 horses and as many mules." These figures are significant only as indicating that there was practically no limit to the amount of such wealth that might be produced. It was simply a question of transportation and a market. Vessels from Mexico or voyaging between there and the Philippines cast anchor at long intervals in our harbor and carried away cargoes of hides and tallow, of wheat and olive oil. Twenty-five years after the Mission of the Bishop there was founded the Mission of San Miguel, four miles south of the northern boundary of the county. Its territory reached far northward and though its operations never quite equalled in magnitude, those of the older establishment, it still accumulated enormous possessions. What the financial results might have been, if instead of the modest ambitions of the saintly Franciscans, the boundless cupidity of a latter day sinful San Franciscan had controlled matters, staggers the imagination. But lacking a market, these large accumulations were lightly valued and were almost common property. It was the agreeable custom of the day that the hungry traveller might slaughter an animal from the nearest herd and it was quite understood that he had entirely met the exigencies of the case if he courteously suspended the hide where the owner of the beast could find it. The hide represented the chief value. And it is only in very recent years that this hospitable notion has been entirely eradicated from the minds of the still existing descendants of those ancient occupants of the land.

CHAPTER III

THE SPANISH REGIME

Nearly two centuries had passed since the landing of Columbus. The horde of adventurers who in the decades immediately following that event had swarmed over the new continent and insane with the lust of gold and conquest had explored it to its limits had passed away and had no successors. The dream of easily acquired and boundless wealth had vanished. Mere land, especially when encumbered with a native population which might at times resent and resist invasion, was not attractive. In the meantime in the northern part of the continent vast changes had taken place. Immigrants from northern Europe had arrived in great numbers. France had acquired a splendid domain in Canada and by the fortunes of war had lost it. The "Thirteen colonies" of England had revolted from the mother country and in them had been born a new nation which in another century was to rank with the most powerful of the earth. The Spanish possessions on the Pacific coast, held for so long by a mere figment of title were gazed at covetously by Russia and by England and their vessels, buccaneer, pirate or privateer ready for any adventure of war or commerce, hovered along these western coasts. If Spain would hold the Californians she must be prepared to defend her rights. She had slept too long upon them.

At this crucial moment, there appeared upon the stage a striking figure, whose name is perhaps less familiar to us than those of his noted subordinates, Father Serra, Governor Portola and Governor Fages, but who really designed and made possible the plans which we have briefly outlined and which were so efficiently carried out. This was Jose de Galvez, the scion of a noble house which for generations had been illustrious but had so diminished that the young Spaniard began his career as a shepherd boy. But his rise was meteoric and he was still young in years but old in political service when he was appointed by his sovereign, Charles III, Visitor-general to New Spain. And while his charge embraced the involved affairs of all the possessions of his country in America, the problems affecting the Californians were the subjects of his special study. As may be gathered from his long and carefully detailed instructions to Father Serra and his other executives, his main motive was the protection of these regions from invasion and the creation of a degree of "preparedness" to resist efforts in that direction which were actually being made. What was especially necessary was population, something difficult to obtain. Spain was by no means overpopulated nor were the Spanish people naturally inclined to emigration. Those among them who were adventurous enough to seek fortune in the new world had nothing in common with the American pioneer and backwoodsman. They were not the material of which settlers could be made. The chief available material was to be found in the native tribes from which laborers could at least be drawn and a forced civilization secured. The end sought was at all events attained. It could not be questioned but that Spain had perfected her title to the Californias by actual and extended occupation. Russia ceased her efforts to extend her possessions southward from Alaska. England could make no claim which would justify her intrusion. Galvez doubtless hoped to realize rich revenues from the development of mines, the creation of a strong and wealth producing dependency in the Californias, but while largely disappointed in these anticipations, he succeeded in establishing there for the next half century, the peaceful and undisturbed dominion of Spain. In the execution of his plans he followed necessarily the ideas evolved by the astute legists of his country. The vast colonial possessions which Spain had acquired in the 16th and 17th centuries, demanded for their exploitation, laws and regulations specially adapted to the conditions arising and the Spanish Laws of Colonization are probably more precise and definite than those of any other modern nation. The conditions were largely the same in most of her colonies. Great expanses of virgin territory never before occupied except by wandering tribes were to be peopled. The missionaries were the pioneers. With a few soldiers to protect them, they made their way through the new country and at convenient intervals established missions, gathered the natives about them, reduced them to semi-civilization and, with their aid built churches and habitations for themselves and such structures as might be required for the instruction and protection of the natives and the storage of the results of their industry. Occasionally there might be a Presidio, a camp of soldiers as a last resort. Finally there were to come civic communities, either evolved from the Missions or growing independently. For the Mission held no title to any lands and could grant none. It had the use of

17

all the vacant territory in its vicinity but after a certain period, supposed to be ten years, it was anticipated that a sufficient white population would have gathered about it, which had to be to the number of fifty, to enable it to become a Pueblo or corporation. On petition to the Governor of the Territory, that civic condition was conferred upon it. Then the whole population came together and named a certain number of electors and these electors proceeded to elect their Ayuntamiento or Common Council, composed of an Alcade or Justice, two Regidores or Aldermen and a Procurador Sindico or City Attorney. Then the town was laid out with a Plaza or public square for centre, then blocks and streets, defining the residence and business lots, then the Ejidos or vacant suburbs which might later become residence property; then the Suertes or cultivatable land, so named because they were distributed to the applicant therefor by lot or chance and thence beyond to the town limits were the Dehesas or common pasture lands. The whole of the lands so described amounted to four square leagues of land and every Pueblo was entitled to that amount upon its creation. The residents then acquired absolute title to their lots or sureties from the Ayuntamiento and the Church buildings and appurtenances were consecrated to religious uses. Title to ranchos was secured in an equally simple manner. There was no money consideration nor apparently any limit to the amount of land granted. It depended upon the capability of the grantee properly to utilize it. A petition was presented to the Governor for the lands desired, setting forth the amount and approximate location, a report was thereupon made by officers deputed to examine the matter and the Governor executed a formal grant accompanied by a rough map of the land which was usually a pen sketch, a few inches square, showing at different points of the compass, noted landmarks, peaks or streams, within which boundary points the land was to be taken. And generally the leagues asked for exhausted all the land of value therein.

But these plans so admirably developed on paper and in the closet curiously failed in actual operation. The strenuous impulse of Galvez and the tireless energy of Serra withdrawn, and both died within a few years, there succeeded an era of simple existence and a progress as gradual as the processes of Nature. Increase of population was hardly noticeable. The natives, from their changed mode of living and the attendant epidemics and the vices and dissipation too readily acquired, diminished in numbers. Immigration was rare. The small force of soldiers at the expiration of their term of enlistment usually remained in the country. Probably they were unable

18

to do otherwise. Perhaps they had no wish to do otherwise. They commonly intermarried with the native girls, found employment and support and were more than contented to remain. The ranks of the soldiery were replenished from Mexico or Spain and the operation was repeated. Many also of the official class and they were quite generally of excellent extraction, became attached to the country and made it their home and their descendants attained distinction here in later days. There were accessions of course to the numbers of the priests. There was ample occupation for them. They were the actual possessors and sole beneficiaries of this vast territory. There were soldiers and their officers but they were the paid retainers of the priests. They enforced order and discipline, pursued and punished the revolted native escaping from his subjection; battled with the wild tribes of the far interior or raided them to gather in fresh material for conversion. And there were government officials in numbers but their jurisdiction did not extend to the funds of the church. And there were no other revenues. It was a golden age of slumberous, measureless content, and its conditions were jealously maintained. The foreigner, intruding by land or sea was an enemy because he was a foreigner particularly if he was not a Catholic and was deported with speed. The scattered community thrilled with anxiety and trepidation when it learned that the great natural barriers of desert and mountain to the east and north had been forced by exploring Gringos, who though few in number and starving and destitute, were still formidable and a menace to their peaceful isolation and their fancied security. It was a contended community and sufficiently prosperous, but it was not the colony of Galvez and under Spain never became so. It was not to be expected. The pueblo implied a population of laborers. Its constitution demanded the humble home of the farmer or herdsman, the parcel of land for cultivation, the common pasture for the cattle. But the labor was free and the laborer independent. But in the California of the Padres, the labor was servile, it was for the Indian. No white man, however debased or degraded, could descend to the level of the native in this direction. For him the proud attitude of the soldier or petty official or looker-on of some kind. So white material was not procurable. The Indian, as a citizen and free-holder was impossible whatever the law might have contemplated. "Carlisle" was not dreamed of in those days and the good priests, Spaniards with Spanish pride of race, could hardly think it possible or even desirable, that their dark-skinned proteges, could be raised by any educational effort to anything like equality in mentality with white men. Ultimately doubtless, had conditions remained unchanged, the requisite native citizen might have appeared. The Indian type gradually liminated in successive generations might have been replaced by a mixed race, able, by virtue of its Spanish strain to gain and guard its personal liberty and through its Indian ancestry content to engage in honest toil. But in the meantime, to hasten the colonization of the country, efforts were made to induce immigration and terms were offered which were apparently liberal. Houses and lots and lands, cattle and horses, tools and implements, food supplies of all kinds were to be furnished the settlers to be repaid from the sale of his crops. Immigrants were sought naturally in the settlement in the Mexican states but the efforts of the Spanish officials, extending over several years, signally failed. After all, considering the conditions, there was nothing attractive in the propositions made. The distance was great and the perils and privations of the journey formidable. California could promise no brighter future for the energetic than could the more settled land of Mexico. In all some twenty families only were induced or compelled to migrate to the new colony and these were of the lowest class, mongrels and vagabonds, a worthless, crew. No further organized effort at immigration appears to have been made by the Spaniards. Doubtless it became speedily evident that the pueblo was impracticable and in view of the success of the padres in grain-raising, unnecessary.

The last decade of Spanish dominion, from 1811 to 1821, was full of anxiety for the scattered inhabitants of California. It had been a time of continuous warfare in Mexico. Perpetual revolt and revolution, desperate efforts of the Spanish armies to quell the uprisings, an endless carnival of bloodshed and destruction had engrossed the attention of the rulers of the distracted country and the outlying territory had been practically abandoned to its own devices. The internecine strife did not reach it. Priests, officials and soldiery were chiefly natives of Spain and intensely loyal to their mother country and had every reason to dread the triumph of the revolutionists and the vital changes that would ensue. It is not improbable, that to the inhabitants of the territory under the Spanish flag, its isolation had been, if not entirely to their liking, at least quite endurable. It is true, it was the "simple life" reduced to its lowest terms. Articles of luxury, fabrics of silk or finery of any kind, manufactures of wood or metal, tools and implements of civilization were obtainable only at long intervals by the small vessels despatched by royal order. But the stricter necessaries of life were abundant. Wheat and maize were plentifully produced. There was no lack of food. Rude looms provided coarse but sufficient clothing. Necessary habitations were easily and cheaply constructed and if there were no roads there were endless bands of horses and mules for all desired uses. There was little necessity or opportunity for strenuous exertion even by the natives. There was ample leisure. In their isolation they were practically independent. It was a far cry to the capital of Mexico and still more remote and unconcerned was the royal authority in Spain. Except for the rare incursions of wandering bands of hostile Indians from the distant interior, poorly armed and easily repulsed, nothing ever occurred to disturb the tranquillity of Spanish California.

While doubtless advised to some extent as to the reverses which the armies of Spain had suffered in their efforts to subdue the revolutionists in Mexico, it was with bitter amazement and dismay that in 1821, Sola, then Governor of California, beheld an armed vessel, under a flag of strange design, anchoring in the bay of Monterey from which ship presently landed an officer who announced himself the accredited representative of his sovereign, Iturbide, Liberator and Emperor of Mexico. A few months later and the wheel of fortune turns again. Iturbide and his Empire have vanished and a new revolution has created the Republic of Mexico. With resignation and rapidity the Californians changed their allegiance. Within the year, they had been subjects of the Kingdom of Spain, the Empire of Mexico and the new Republic.

To the padres, the change of government was a dire menace. It was not alone that they were natives of Spain and resolute to maintain their allegiance to their mother country. Had they been Mexican priests of the stamp of Hidalgo, their tenure would have been equally precarious. Captives to the Mexican rulers, they were in the hands of their enemies who while nominally Catholic, accepting the tenets of a loosely held faith were densely ignorant, vicious and revengeful and attributing the evils which had moved them to revolt and the dire cruelties to which the Mexican natives had been subjected for more than three centuries to priestly influence were naturally bent upon its dimunition or destruction. And it was not alone this hostility to their office which excited the grave apprehensions of the friars. In their charge and custody was the wealth of the country and it might be deemed a certainty that these bandit officials forced by the desperate destitution of the Republican treasury and restrained by no religious compunctions or terror of priestly reprisal would not hesitate to loot the

21

sacred accumulations of the Missions. Their fears were well-founded.

Some little delay however ensued. The cupidity of the Mexican officials was held in check by their conviction that under the existing conditions the immediate ouster of the padres would result in cessation of agricultural production to their own grave detriment. From a purely selfish standpoint, the retention, for a time at least of the machinery of the Missions was imperatively necessary. So the new rulers contented themselves with absorbing the revenues of the Church whenever they could find a pretext to do so and with persistent efforts to induce the priests to accept allegiance to the new government. In most cases the Mission fathers were utterly recalcitrant. Many of them were ultimately banished and some fled to escape worse persecution. Among the latter was Father Luis Antonio Martinez, the incumbent of the Mission of San Luis Obispo. It is related that he succeeded in sending to his Superiors in Spain as much of the wealth of the Mission as he could convert into specie and after suffering many things from the government officials at last escaped from their hands and reached his mother country in safety.

Conceding as is but just, that the Mission fathers, during the six decades of their rule had been faithfully following the foot steps of their great leader, endeavoring to realize the vision of Serra of a multitude of souls redeemed from pagan worship and heathendom, it must have been with infinite sorrow and distress that they contemplated the coming destruction of the work of their hands. Their ideal had been reached. In three or four generations, the poor aborigines, survivors of the stone age, had been measurably raised in the scale of civilization. They had been brought to accept the Christian faith, they had been taught habits of industry and instructed in handicrafts and had become as sheep in the hands of their shepherd. If now they were to be deprived of their guardians and protectors, thrown out upon the world, the hirelings of unfeeling strangers, who would have no interest in their spiritual, moral or material welfare, was it not inevitable that they would relapse into barbarism or meet a still worse fate? The zeal and devotion, the prayers and teachings of the bands of earnest missionaries would have been wasted.

In a lesser degree, it must also have exasperated Father Martinez to see the coffers of the Church robbed of the wealth with which he and his predecessors and co-workers had filled them. All the cattle upon a thousand hills; the barns and storehouses bursting

22

with grain, the wine and olive oil and various products which had been reckoned as religious funds were now to be taken and squandered in the support of a mongrel crew of officials. And still another source of profound regret was that he must be exiled from this, the loveliest of all the Missions. As we have said, the buildings themselves lacked in a degree that architectural beauty which has become so typically Californian. They resembled quite closely those of the Mission Dolores, built some four yeears later and like them have a quiet dignity which is impressive. The ancient structures are not so greatly changed to this day in spite of the ravages of time during the century and a half of years which they have survived and the dubious efforts at preservation which they have withstood. In its original surroundings the Mission must have been exceedingly attractive. Perched upon a slight eminence, with its long stretch of white walls and red-tiled roofs, the towering facade of the church, pierced and recessed for its bells and surmounted by its cross, it was a striking feature of the landscape. The church itself was the usual long and narrow building for it would seem that the good fathers were not familiar with the principle of the truss or were unable to apply it so the width of the church was dependent on the length of the rafters, laid from the side walls to the ridge pole. The interior decorations were crude and the paintings somewhat archaic. Our Mission was not one of those favored with original Murillos. The central feature of the Mission was its garden, surrounded on all sides by buildings for the various uses of the institution and fronting with the church extended the main buildings designed for the accommodation of the priests and the demands of hospitality. Along the front of these buildings ran an arcade which was picturesque and pleasurable. Fronting the east it received the rays of the morning sun and afforded shelter from the afternoon winds from the ocean. Immediately before it ran the road or trail, dignified by the name of the Camino Real along which came all the travellers through the territory. Along the road ran the arroyo and beyond for a half mile in width, stretched the "Gardens," bounded on the further side by low hills and extending still further north and south. And then on to the horizon in the south was a view of a Delectable land. The "Gardens," as described covered many acres, a level tract of deep rich alluvial in which growth was luxurious and perpetual. Here had been nurtured all the choicest growths of the orchards and gardens and vineyards of old Spain, olive and fig, orange and lemon, pomegranate and grape, the whole category in short of fruit, flower and vegetable. Artistically laid out, laboriously cared for and abundantly watered, the gardens were of surpassing beauty. Fifty years later, the streets and buildings of the city had obliterated all trace of the Gardens, but in odd corners so many of the old olive trees of the padres still remained that the town was fain to style itself the "City of the Olive." Such was the scene which rendered so agreeable the promenade in the Arcade of the Mission. But times change and conditions change with them. The Camino Real no longer skirts the walls of the Mission. Uninteresting buildings across the street block the view. And when in process of time the pillars of the arcade began to crumble, the resident fathers, preferring the full sunshine to the shadow of the arcade, consented to its removal.

While some of the minor buildings, no longer needed, fell at last to decay, much of the construction was of a permanent character. Some of the granite walls, laid up in cement are still standing and very much in the way. Nothing but dynamite will disintegrate them and the composition of the cement is a matter of curious speculation. Tradition affirms that the "blood of bulls" was an ingredient! At all events the old Mission still competently fulfilling its destiny, bids fair to stand for centuries to come, an enduring monument of the days when Father Martinez was driven from it and of the noble work to which the Padres consecrated their lives.

Whatever of good resulted ultimately from the political changes which followed so rapidly, however inadequate we may consider the efforts of the missionaries to civilize the natives, our sympathies must be stirred at the spectacle of the disconsolate priests sadly departing from the scenes of their long labors and lamenting the frustration of their hopes and plans.

CHAPTER IV

MEXICAN RULE AND MISRULE

To the downfall of the Spanish dominion in Mexico and the dependent territory, California submitted with fear and dismay. The long struggle of the Mexicans for independence had, in this distant section excited but little interest and had certainly created no sympathy. That was to be expected. Aside from the natives and the mongrel population bred from them the Californians were chiefly Spaniards by birth or of recent Spanish extraction and intensely proud of the fact. Priests and officials were direct from Spain and the other people of standing and prominence in the colony were all of the same race. They had no tyranny to complain of, no reason for disloyalty. Their existence, the settlement of the colony, its continued security, its support when needed, were due to the mother country. The rulers sent them were men of race. The iron hand might be there but it was sheathed in the velvet glove. They felt themselves an integral, important and highly regarded part of their own country. Now they were a conquered people, in the power of their enemies, subject to the rule of satraps sent to exploit them and from whose edicts there was no appeal. After the glittering vision of untold wealth, of gold and pearls and precious stones which had lured the early navigators and explorers had proven but a "base fabric," the keen interest of Spain in the Californias practically ceased. Other parts of her vast possessions absorbed her efforts at exploitation. When finally it became necessary to define and defend her ownership, the plans developed by Galvez indicate little expectation of wealth to be gained. The chief design was to people the new territory and if possible to make it self-supporting. Its inhabitants were to be purely Spanish and to have no relation commercially or otherwise with other nations. No foreign vessels were permitted to land on its shores and no foreigners were allowed to visit it. And these conditions maintained, as they were, very willingly and thoroughly, the peaceful security of the peoples was rarely troubled by official regulation, by the visit of the tax-gatherer or interference with personal liberty.

Now in the new regime came a lamentable change. The rulers sent them from Mexico were as little Spanish as possible. Tyrannical and suspicious, they intensified the odium in which they would naturally have been held and in the fifteen years of their sway they made California, politically another Mexico, seething with revolt and with rivals in its leadership in every considerable hamlet. The only Mexican Governor whose record appears creditable was Jose Figueroa, who served from January, 1833, to August, 1835. He was of a purer race, chiefly Aztec. And it was to him that was entrusted the task of the secularization of the Missions.

This much debated measure was without doubt launched by the Mexican government with the object of looting the accumulations of the Church. It was hardly to be expected that the lean and hungry victors should neglect such easy spoil. By the laws of Spain, the Missions had only the right of temporary use of all the vast areas they occupied. The sovereign of the country could dispossess them at will and the sovereign was now Mexico. And by an easy construction of law, the other various forms of wealth held by the priests and produced under their management was the property of the kingdom and the successor in ownership was the Republic. If legal justification was required, it could be produced. But the emissaries of Mexico, charged with the execution of the decree of secularization were not concerned as to its legality.

It was rather the brutal and tyrannical execution of the Decree than the measure itself which is to be criticised. But yet had the duty been assigned to a grandee of Spain, a devoted son of the Church, while the humiliation of the padres might have been spared them, the results would not have been materially different. Such an executive would have exercised the diplomacy and polished courtesy of his race and rank and while restricting the temporal possessions of the Church to the Mission buildings and lands immediately appurtenant, he would have held those possessions sacred and from the moiety of the personalty assured them in the law, he might have established an endowment which would have richly provided for their needs and that of their Indian wards for all time. Whatever might have been the intent of the Mexican government a fair construction of the terms of the Decree of Secularization dictates precisely that course. It was a natural sequence of the Colonization laws of Spain to which we have referred under which Galvez had acted. Under different conditions they might have been successful. As for instance, with a sufficient population of stolid, laborious, unambitious, Church-fearing Spanish peasantry.

No such population was attainable. To such ideal material the native Indian was a violent contrast.

But however benevolent and paternal the law was in appearance, wide-spread disaster followed its enforcement. The initial step to be taken under the law was the taking possession by government agents of all the properties held by the Church. But when the day appointed arrived, those possessions had practically disappeared. With a besom of destruction, the priests had taken their revenge. Only dismantled and deserted church buildings remained. Granaries and warehouses had been swept clean of their contents and wrecked and ruined. Trees and vines, the growth of a half century had been cut down, torn up and destroyed. Fires had laid waste the cultivated fields and the air was heavy with the pestilential odors from the carcasses of the great herds of cattle, left where they fell, a prey to the buzzards and wild animals. The general butchery had been easily accomplished by the division of the booty of the hides and tallow. The triumph of the priests was complete but it was to them discreditable and disastrous. In the ensuing years, other priests succeeded them and while the church edifices remained undisturbed in their sacred uses, the appurtenant buildings and enclosed lands passed to strangers to be regained only after long delay. Only after the American occupation and ownership was the title of the Church confirmed to the fifty acres or so that the Mission fathers had actually enclosed and cultivated. And for the time being at least, the priests in charge were without support. The Mother Church could give but little assistance. The Mexican government certainly had no disposition to do so and the congregations were not as yet organized for their support. The priests suffered greatly. It is even stated that in some parts of the territory they actually starved.

The unfortunate natives were perhaps the chief sufferers by the destruction of the Missions. They were freed at last from the servitude of generations but they were deprived as well of the masters who had guided their destinies, directed their labors and ensured their support. Once again they were wanderers and less capable of self support than were their remote ancestors. Time at last solved their problem. Many attached themselves to the ranch owners who presently spread over the country, many wended their way inland, joined the yet wild tribes and reverted to their original conditions while still others sunk in vice and destitution, herded together in the vicinity of the white settlements and gradually perished. Fifty years later there was not an Indian in the county.

The last traces discoverable of the tribes once so numerous was in the darker skin or coarser features of an occasional Mexican.

The territory about San Luis Obispo remained placid and undisturbed through all the tribulation and disorder of the Mexican rule. The salient feature of that rule, the dominant motive was cupidity, and here there was nothing to exploit. As a province of Spain, California was not overburdened with wealth but there was no distress, no complaint. The white population was homogeneous. The civil and military authorities were the countrymen and except perhaps for some occasional personal disagreement, the cordial friends of the priests and shared with them the bounty that Nature granted to the toil of their numerous retainers. If greater bounty was desired and an added number of retainers or some display of force to induce their more active exertion, the soldiery gladly shared the common task, scouring the wilds for more Indians or effectively disciplining those in hand. With the advent of the Mexican governors, this dolce far niente life vanished. Those gentry encountered an empty treasury and no effort of theirs was ever successful in satisfactorily filling it. Not for them the fraternal aid of the padres. On the contrary, the products of the Missions steadily declined, the natives diminished in numbers, levies upon the Church funds were evaded upon the plea of poverty which was doubtless justified even though in a large measure wilfully created. Which being the case, other resources must be sought. Commerce could be encouraged and revenues derived from duties. So the Spanish regulations permitting no foreign vessel to land were abrogated and American droghers and British and Russian traders became frequent visitors. And duties ranging in the vicinity of fifty per cent ad valorem were productive of considerable revenue despite the smuggling which the exorbitant customs invited and by which some of the customs officers were not too scrupulous to profit. With the "open door" for commercial relations with the world, came the final evolution, the wholesale reduction of the public lands to private ownership, resulting from the extinguishment of the claims of the Missions to exclusive possession.

Among the civilians or soldiers sent to serve in California by the Spanish authorities, there were some who from choice or the force of circumstances became permanent residents. Many of these inherited a high degree of intelligence and culture and could rightfully trace relationship to families of high degree in their native country. They constituted a considerable number of the Europeans in the new territory and in the course of time by constant inter-marriage, became a strong and influential body. When under the Mexican flag, hostility to foreigners practically ceased there began to arrive in increasing numbers, Americans and Englishmen, young, energetic and ambitious, who presently found wives among the beautiful and highbred senoritas and these families added mate-rially to the strength and numbers of this quasi aristocracy. We say numbers advisedly. Those early Spanish-American grandees exulted in their numerous progeny. Bancroft in his History says that Senora De Haro informed him that she had been the mother of twenty-five children. Which we fancy is a record or a mistake.

When, therefore, it become the policy of the Mexican authorities to distribute the lands of the territory to those who had the ability to replace the padres in their effective use, it was naturally to this wealthier and abler class that the Mexican governors appealed. Doubtless little urging was required. In the decade which remained of Mexican rule vast acres passed to private ownership. As an instance, in San Luis Obispo county, one of the first grants was made to an American, William C. Dana, a son of the famous Boston family of that name who had established himself in business in Santa Barbara in 1825; three years later he had married the eldest daughter of Carrillo the Governor of the Territory and in 1835 was granted a tract of his selection, comprising about 40,000 acres. Many other Americans were similarly obliged and obliging and others secured by purchase from Spanish or Mexican grantees, lands which they could not themselves obtain from by grant. In all, the "Spanish grants" so-called, in this county aggregated about a half a million acres.

Probably at the time this apparent squandering of the public domain was a wise policy. These princely estates, which in a few years were to be of great value, were then comparatively worthless. If the grantees could have found purchasers it would have been at a few cents only per acre. The "improvements" they erected, frequently large and commodious but of cheap and rude material and workmanship, far exceeded the land in value. And the expec-tations of the government were generally realized. The energy and ability of the grantees speedily dwarfed the achievements of the padres and wealth and population rapidly increased. So inter-related, the Spanish families became a tribe, having a common heredity and the ties of race were strengthened by those of mutual interest. Life was simple, patriarchal and primitive, joyous and carefree. There was abundance without strenuous effort to secure it and it was generously shared. Every chief had his numerous body of retainers and dependents. He was a feudal lord in miniature.

The period of Mexican rule in California was merely an interregnum which was manifestly destined to end as it did, in the absorption of the territory by America. Mexico had contributed to its population only a scanty proportion and that generally of the most debased and worthless character and while the Californians severed forever from their mother country, Spain, were compelled to share the fortunes of the other Mexican provinces in their successful revolt, it was with no good will. They were "tories" and the ill fortune which continually dogged the footsteps of all the rulers sent from Mexico to govern them was mainly due to their latent hostility. In fact, in 1837, the hostility became so pronounced that there was a revolt headed by Juan B. Alvarado, one of the ablest of the Californians. Gutierrez, the Governor at the time, was driven out of the country and California declared itself an independent nation. What kind of a nation never developed. It was perhaps an oligarchy. It lasted but a short time and was diplomatically ended by the appointment of Alvarado himself as Governor by the Mexican authorities. But if California was unequal to the task of maintaining an independent existence it continued to be restless under the sway of Mexico and there were manifestations of a desire for incorporation either with England or America. Union with the latter was to be speedily attained. For political reasons, the national administration of the United States welcomed a war with Mexico. In the event of American victory, which was probable, we might expect to acquire all the vast northern possessions of Mexico in which California would be included. The war did occur and with the hoped for results. So far as this section of the country was concerned, there was no reason why the transfer of government should not have been as uneventful as was the case when Mexico achieved her independence. The native Californians were predisposed to accept union with the American republic. In the decade preceding the close of the Mexican war there had been considerably increased immigration of Americans, hunters and trappers, explorers and adventurers, and pioneers with their families, afflicted with wanderlust seeking new lands. Most of these were from the then Western frontier states along the Mississippi, a sturdy, stalwart, independent class, whose descendants were to figure largely in the upbuilding of the new state. Their good qualities rarely included much culture or refinement however.

30

Their speech was an Americanese of their own and they were apt to view with suspicion and distaste and to regard as identical all language differing from theirs whether Castilian or Indian. A complexion darker than their own, forced itself upon their minds as denoting an inferior race, to be generally characterized as "greaser." Accustomed to "squat" on any uncultivated land that took their fancy, they did not take kindly to the idea that one man could monopolize vast areas and exclude therefrom the honest settler. Courts and peace officers were busied for years in forcibly altering their point of view. And their habitations were not decorative. The writer has a joyous memory of hearing General Vallejo voice his disgust, flavored with appropriate expletives, at the mansion of one of the "Pikes." That was the generic name for all that class of immigrants, whether coming from that famous county in "Mizzourah" or not. We were riding by the shack in question, a characteristic one, clumsily put together of boards and shakes, already rickety and dilapidated, and while it might charitably be considered picturesque, its general air of shiftlessness fully justified the ire of the progressive Spanish grandee. But that was some years after California became American territory. During the transition period and until the war with Mexico began, they were unwelcome intruders but being more than willing to lend their assistance with their trusty rifles to any faction leader who raised a banner of revolt and with no over-nicety as to the cause of the quarrel they inspired respect and gained tolerance. They, of course, were more than ready to fight to make California American territory. There was in short nothing to "conquer." Whatever disturbances were created resulted from hysterical efforts of American "conquistadores" to immortalize their names. In 1842, Commodore Ap Catesby Jones, commanding the U. S. man-of-war United States landed at Monterey, took the fort, hoisted the American flag and demanded from the astonished authorities immediate surrender of all the Californias. He had been informed that war had been declared between Mexico and the United States. The next day he hauled down the flag, apologized and sailed away much abashed. He had received later and more correct information. On July 2, 1846, another U. S. man-of-war, commanded by Commodore Sloat, anchored at Monterey and after some hesitation, remembering the unlucky exploit of Jones and really having no more certain information than had Jones, he on the 7th of the month took possession of the government buildings and again the flag was raised. This time it was to stay, but Sloat departed, turning over the command to Commodore Stockton. On the 13th of January, 1847, the treaty of Cahuenga was signed by which it was agreed that all opposition to the American occupation should cease and thereafter peace reigned.

San Luis Obispo maintained an attitude of benevolent neutrality during these later days of turmoil. Her chief families were a due and equal admixture of American and Spanish-Californian blood. Partisanship under the circumstances was inadvisable and unnecessary and the horrid front of war was not seen on her soil except on the memorable occasion when the gallant Fremont bravely captured her chief city and came near shooting the amiable Jose de Jesus Pico. The future near-President was on his way southward with a band of "Pikes" and Walla-Walla Indians. The city of San Luis Obispo consisted then of a score of one-story adobe buildings scattered along the highway near the Mission. It was a dark and stormy November midnight when the Americanos neared the doomed city sunk in peaceful slumber. Then with wild yells and galloping furiously, they dashed on to brilliant victory. It detracted somewhat from its brilliancy that there was nothing to surrender and nobody authorized to do it if there had been, and the army was uncomfortably wet. As many as could find room, however, crowded into the old church and the priests' quarters. With true martial instinct, Fremont proceeded to intrench himself and his men threw up a breastwork on a lot overlooking the city. As for certain reasons the lot has never been built upon, the half-filled trenches are still traceable and are pointed out to admiring tourists as Fremont's Fort. A few days later the troops departed to seek the elusive foe. Señor Pico, above-mentioned, was a cousin of Andreas Pico, one of the Spanish leaders. He had been previously captured and released on parole. He had sheathed the sword all right, but he had drawn the pen as it appeared, he having written a private letter to a friend, in which he spoke harshly of the bad habit of the Americans of commandeering cattle and horses and other personal property without regard to the wishes or rights of their owners. This evil conduct in the opinion of Fremont constituted a breach of parole which required his immediate death. But his dread fate was happily averted through the influence, it is said, of a delegation of ladies of much personal charm. Pico was not only freed, but accompanied Fremont on his departure and was of great assistance in the negotiations which shortly followed between the American leader and the Spanish-Californians and which permanently ended their armed opposition to the American occupation.

Fremont might have been neither a great statesman nor a brilliant warrior, but he had the gift of achieving popularity and his success in that direction with the Californians was extraordinary. A few months after his spectacular performance at San Luis Obispo, he had occasion to pass through the village again and nothing could exceed the enthusiasm with which he was received by the whole population of the country thereabouts. It was due doubtless to his personal magnetism and to the magnanimity displayed in his treatment of their compatriots.

Fremont's passage through San Luis Obispo referred to was in the course of his celebrated ride from Los Angeles to Monterey and back again, a distance of 840 miles, which he accomplished in the running time of seventy-six hours. The performance was the more remarkable as the journey was over rough trails and through a mountainous country. He was accompanied only by his friend Pico and a servant, Jacob Dodson, each having three horses, riding one for twenty miles, then changing to another. It was quite a wonderful deed, demonstrating the physical powers of both horses and riders, but if it was undertaken for any special reason it is nowhere recorded. There would seem to have been no political cause for such headlong haste. Fremont had been appointed Governor of California by Commodore Stockton, at the moment the ranking United States officer in the territory, but his authority was almost at once challenged by Gen. S. W. Kearny, who arrived very inopportunely, from Washington with a commission in his pocket, conferring that distinguished honor upon him. Fremont was governing from Los Angeles and Kearny from Monterey. Kearny summoned Fremont to Monterey and then ordered his immediate return and the "ride" was in pursuance of those orders but not the order of his going.

In June, 1849, San Luis Obispo was created one of the ten districts into which, by order of Governor Bennett Riley, the Territory of California was divided from which to elect delegates to a convention which he called for the purpose of framing a constitution for the new state which was to be thereby created. The election was held on August 1st, the delegates chosen from San Luis Obispo being Henry A. Tefft and Jose M. Covarrubias. The convention met at Monterey on September 1st and adjourned on the 13th of October and on the 13th of November the constitution so framed was submitted to a vote of the people and adopted by a vote of 12,064 in its favor to 811 against it. The constitution defined the boundaries of the new state as well as the counties into which it was to be divided as also the assembly and senatorial districts. San Luis Obispo was constituted an assembly district and it and Santa Barbara were made a senatorial district. Tefft was the first assemblyman elected from this district and Don Pablo de la Guerra of Santa Barbara, the first senator. The Legislature met on the 15th of December and the self-constituted state entered upon its career without waiting for the consent of Congress which, however, was accorded on the 9th of September in the following year. San Luis Obispo was an important part of the state territorially but hardly so in point of population. The census of 1850 gave it but 336 inhabitants.

CHAPTER V

AMERICAN TERRITORY

By the confirmation by Congress of the political action of the people of the State of California, San Luis Obispo became a political entity, endowed with all the appurtenant rights and privileges thereof and proceeded to carve out its own destiny. The population was largely Spanish and that language was in general if not exclusive use, and in the first elections held the candidates were frequently Spanish. The early records of the county were kept in that language and court proceedings conducted in it. If the services of an interpreter were required, it was for the benefit of recent arrivals who had not yet acquired the native speech. To these newcomers the local laws and regulations were strange and unfamiliar. The ruling body of the county was a court consisting of a Judge and two Justices of the Peace, who were endowed with all the legislative, executive and judicial functions needed. in their judgment, for the public welfare. If any one committed an act which was against the peace and dignity of the commonwealth, the court defined the crime, affixed the penalty and had it enforced. If imprisonment was impracticable, he might be given into the custody of some county dignitary to work out the penalty. Were roads required, the court ordered the laying out and construction thereof and provided for their future upkeep, and if need be directed that "the people of the county be summoned without delay to mend the roads of the county." Nothing in short was too large or too small to escape its attention. It had final jurisdiction of land squabbles, created a "pale" for the Indians who were not yet all extinct, directed that all cattle should be killed on certain ground appropriated for the purpose and not elsewhere in the vicinity of the town, limited the number of cattle that each person should have the right to pasture on the public lands, required the registration of all "strangers" on their arrival and, in short, assumed all the powers of a state except to coin money or declare war. The padres had in their time constructed a dam and irrigating ditch which diverted the water from its natural channel in the San Luis Obispo Creek

35

and carried it through the present townsite. An excellent enterprise then, but in the course of time there were disastrous results to follow. The mother stream finally followed the ditch, and floods widened and deepened the stream, until costly bridges and retaining walls were in later years rendered necessary. But in the days of the court, the "canals" were of vast importance to those who had succeeded to the "right of water" and so a superintendent was appointed to distribute the water and compel the owners to do their respective parts in making due repairs, and with power to impose fines for disobedience to their orders.

Cattle-raising being the great industry of the county, special legislation was demanded for its protection, and a number of the more prominent citizens were created "Judges of the Plains," with quite manifold duties. Some one of them had to attend all "rodeos," of which there were some thirty every year in different parts of the county. These were round-ups of all the cattle in the vicinity and the branding and marking of all young cattle, without which the ownership could not be determinel. Then, too, when cattle were butchered, some Judge of the Plains must be advised and ascertain that the animals were properly branded and vented, in other words, the rightful property of the butcher. And another important duty for the Judge of the Plains was to accompany every band of cattle passing through the county and satisfy himself that the drover had no cattle in his herd except such as he had a bill of sale for, or some other evidence of good title. This was highly essential. As there were no fenced roads, the great bands of cattle, driven from the southern part of the state to supply the northern populations, spread over the pasture lands of the county and without great precaution the cattle of the county would be swept into the drover's herd and carried along with it. It was not always by accident.

This rather picturesque government, however, was of but short duration. In 1852 the Legislature provided for Boards of Supervisors in this and other counties of the state, and the manner of local government became practically the same as in other counties in the Union. The earlier party predilection of the voters was with the Whigs. There was a large majority in favor of General Scott in the Presidential election of 1852, and for Fremont in 1856. But the multiplicity of national parties was shared in the county in the years preceding the Civil war so that Lincoln failed of a majority in 1860, but thereafter, for several successive Presidential elections, the Republicans were in the majority. But in the minor elections, party fealty weighed but little at any time, a characteristic by the way which still persists. Personal popularity, the appeal of family or friendship, or sympathy, has always decided the election. Repeatedly, the returns have shown a flattering majority for the candidate of one party, and an equally large vote in favor of the nominee of his political opponents for some other office. No more apt illustration of which could be given than the showing made in the election of 1916. The registration showed that 4,791 of the voters of the county had registered as Republicans; 2,980 male and 1,911 female; 2,681 as Democrats, 1,636 male and 1,045 female; 1,124 as Non-Partisans, 583 males, 541 females; 455 as Socialists, 304 males and 151 females; 199 as Progressives, 110 males and 89 females, and 162 Prohibitionists, 37 males and 125 females. In all 9,412, 5,650 male and 3,762 female. Practically the registration was two to one Republican; 6,383 votes were cast. The Republican candidate for the Assembly had a majority of 1,276, but the Democratic candidate for the State Senate had 2,380 votes more than his Republican opponent. E. A. Hayes, the Republican candidate for Congress, had a majority of 2,499 and Hiram Johnson, Republican nominee for U. S. Senate, 1,614, and yet the Democratic Presidential electors carried the county by 675. Perhaps the vote for the Woodrow Wilson electors and for Governor Johnson might be omitted from this illustration as irrelevant. The circumstances, it will be remembered, were peculiar. The State of California itself gave Governor Johnson the colossal majority of over 300,000 and at the same time gave the casting vote by a majority of 3,200 for the Democratic candidate for President. But as to the other aspirants for office the normal condition obtains, the party label controls not at all. It is the land of the independent voters and all forms of political faith have their adherents. Much of this independence results doubtless from the heterogeneous character of the population. Coming from widely varying environments, they are cast in different moulds, have different comprehension of the meaning of words and the trend of events, and accustomed now to entire freedom of action within the law in all other affairs, they have all confidence in the accuracy of their political judgment and look for the guidance of no leader. Which argues well for the future of the community. The rising generation will follow in their independent course but perhaps with wider knowledge and keener comprehension.

The Spanish strain of the earliest days is still, not infrequently encountered. It is singular that it should be so, considering the small number of those first occupants of the land and that there have been few if any accessions to the population from old Spain in the intervening century or more. Next after the Spaniards in peopling the county came Americans, largely from the New England states and New York, but in lesser numbers from all parts of the United States. After the Civil war, quite a number came to the county from the Southern states. And up to that time, the population was almost exclusively American or Spanish-Californian. Since then many immigrants have come here from Switzerland, mostly from the Canton of Ticino; many Portuguese, natives of the Azore Islands, numbers too of Swedes, Danes and Norwegians. These form the bulk of the foreign-born population. Generally they are farmers and dairymen. Although it is probably true that as a rule they brought nothing with them but youth and strength and hope, yet with their inborn habits of industry and economy, and spurred on by the golden opportunities offered for financial success, many have become wealthy and failure has been rare. By which should be understood that notwithstanding the handicap of a strange language and environment they have quite fully shared the common lot of kindly fortune. In fact the American element has seemed the less permanent. A list made of the American-born citizens who twenty-five years ago were the leaders in the town of San Luis Obispo, its chief lawyers and doctors and business men, included about sixty names. All of these men were apparently prosperous, few of them were unmarried. They quite generally owned their homes. They gave permanency and stability to the town. They filled the offices, the chairs in the lodges, the committees in conventions and public meetings. They constituted apparently the life of the town, civilly, politically and socially. It might be expected that they and their descendants for generations to come would retain that position of commanding influence. Today not one person upon that list remains here and not one of them has left a descendant or representative to bear his name. All are dead or removed. A new people occupy the places which they vacated.

With the election of the Board of Supervisors in 1852, San Luis Obispo entered in earnest upon the business of being a county. Until that time, the governing body, the Court of Sessions, had combined legislative, judicial and executive functions with at times farcical results. Relieved of legal and police responsibility, the Supervisors speedily systematized the business of the community and began the march of improvement. It appears that in January of the epochal year, the treasury was empty and the county owed about $1,300. The tax rate was fifty cents on the one hundred dollars. The real estate assessed was almost entirely ranch property and the total value thereof, together with the improvements thereon amounted to $263,926, being at the rate of fifty cents an acre or less, while the personal property, chiefly live stock, was appraised at $196,604, a total of $460,530. This throws light upon the popular estimate of values in those days. For taxable purposes, probably, the assessment was about one-half of what was considered the full value of the property, real or personal. Five years later the tax rate had increased to $2.20 per hundred but the assessment roll remained about the same, $466,870.50. In 1859, however, the ranch lands rose suddenly in taxable value. The Supervisors, sitting as a Board of Equalization determined upon a scale of valuation, related to the character of the land and its accessibility and listed the ranchos of the county in four classes accordingly, valued respectively at $1.25; $1.00; seventy-five and fifty cents per acre. Upon this rating, the Assessor made up his list which then aggregated, for real and personal property, $1,030,352.75. In 1862-3-4, however, the valuation had to be greatly reduced. Those were years of drouth, unprecedented, and which have never since recurred. It afflicted all southern California and more especially the stock-raisers. In San Luis Obispo, the cattle were almost entirely destroyed. The reduction from this cause and the depreciation in land values greatly diminished the assessable values. The total county assessment for 1864 was only $545,210.

In 1875, however, the assessment roll of the county was $5,332,-784. During the interval, population had largely increased, government land had been taken up and occupied and large ranchos subdivided and sold to settlers. The acreage upon the assessment roll had increased from 537,457 acres in 1852 to 991,404. This increased occupation had involved the necessity of constructing roads and bridges, a costly business in so wide a territory and rendered still more costly by the methods employed and the lack of science and system displayed. Other considerable expenditures had been necessary, among them the building of a county hospital and of a Court house, the latter costing $42,000. The tax money had not been adequate to meet all these disbursements and a bonded debt had been incurred amounting to $157,000. These bonds bore interest at the rate of eight and ten per cent per annum, that being customary at the time of their issuance. However in 1883, conditions had changed in the money market and the Supervisors found no difficulty in issuing and selling new bonds bearing interest at the rate of five per cent with the proceeds of which they bought up and cancelled the earlier issues.

But while at times the financial affairs of the county presented problems during the first decade of its existence which were difficult of solution, a still more difficult one was the uprooting and destroying of a criminal element which had fastened upon it. This demanded strenuous exertion and required the utmost efforts of all the officials, ably assisted by a Vigilance committee in which was enrolled most of the prominent citizens of the county, Spanish and American. During those years there was a reign of criminal violence throughout California. It was a transition period. Government was feeble, courts were powerless and the lax administration of the law bred crime. There was a conflict of races and the vicious and indolent Mexican peons and half-breeds, who chiefly constituted the dangerous classes, found little consideration at the hands of the rough white element and without doubt were often treated with injustice and cruelty. Impelled by a spirit of revenge or lust for crime, there were bands of these wretches who roamed the country, robbing and murdering where they could do so with impunity and they pursued their reckless career for several years until they were exterminated. Many were killed in conflicts with the officers of the law, some were imprisoned for long terms or were executed for their crimes and others fled the country. But for a time they terrorized the community. San Luis Obispo was a favorite resort of these bandits. Two of their most dreaded leaders, Joaquin Murietta and Tiburcio Vasquez, frequently camped here. The conditions were ideal for their criminal purposes. The scanty population was scattered on the great ranchos, at haciendas miles apart. Through the county and stretching along the coast from Monterey to Los Angeles there were continuous chains of mountains and in the deep canyons and gorges was concealment and security. From their secluded dens the robbers descended upon the occasional travelers along the lonely coast road or raiding the ranchos, ran off cattle and horses through secret mountain trails north, east and south. But there were sterling qualities in the pioneer Americans and Spaniards of the county and their courage and determination speedily ended the era of organized crime in this section of the state.

CHAPTER VI

TRAVEL AND TRANSPORTATION

Had it been a question of describing the roads of the County of San Luis Obispo as they existed twenty-two years after the Legislature of the State of California had formally created the county and just a century after Padre Serra had founded the Mission, the faithful historian might naturally have recalled the famous chapter on Snakes in Ireland or the solemn conclusion of the countryman, who for the first time beheld the giraffe. As in those classic instances, he might have denied the existence of any "sich animile." Father Palou, indeed, in his life of Padre Junipero Serra, after describing the fortunate location of the Mission, distant, he says, three leagues from Buchon Bay, where the natives caught savory fish for the padres and where the schooner came at long intervals bringing their supplies, wrote that between the Mission and the bay, there was a "good road." But that only meant that through the open valley and down the canyon through which ran to the ocean, the Arroyo of San Luis Obispo, nature had interposed no obstacles to travel which would be regarded as such by the stately Spanish mule or the little Mexican burro, which were the beasts of burden for the good padres and carried their exports of hides and horns and tallow to the schooner and brought back the longed-for supplies. But if not a road, technically speaking, it was at least a highway, a trail that had existed for countless ages. It ran from the ocean to the "cuesta" or pass in the Santa Lucia Range, the most feasible crossing of those mountains in the county and was the natural route for the wild creatures, two- or four-footed, in their wanderings between the sea and the interior. When the great ranchos were created, similar trails connected their widely distant centers and ran to the old Mission and were even marked by the wheel tracks of the stout "caretas" with their ponderous running gear and poles, propelled by oxen, their yokes firmly lashed behind their wide-spread horns. And even long after the "gringos" came, bringing with them vehicles of all sorts, the wheel tracks across the open unfenced country, even when as was at times the case, they followed in the same ruts could hardly be considered

41

a road. Perhaps even at the present writing, the same conditions may be found in remote corners of the county. Roads which are duly surveyed and mapped and dedicated to the public use but are not yet enclosed or "worked" and where every mile or two a cross fence is encountered, furnished with a gate which the traveller is obliged to open and which it is still more obligatory that he should close after him. But these are conditions common to all undeveloped countries and in this county are rapidly disappearing. At the time to which we have referred, in 1872, they were general. The lands were still held in large bodies and were of small value and the expense of constructing even main trunk lines was formidable. In this year however systematic road work was commenced. Authorized by the State Legislature, the supervisors imposed a road tax and bonds were issued to the amount of $15,000. With the proceeds, a road was constructed from the county seat along the coast to San Simeon and from the northern to the southern boundary of the county.

This last mentioned one followed, because it could not do otherwise, the line of the more lately famous "Camino Real," the Royal Road or King's Highway. The high-sounding name related rather to the King's couriers and messengers by whom it was chiefly used than to its regal perfection as a road. Although Father Palou's "good road" of which we have spoken, in its extension to the Cuesta, the primeval trail, was to become a section of the Camino Real, Don Gaspar de Portola, commanding in 1769, the first exploring party to traverse the county, passed it unnoticed. He was on his "path of glory," the farther terminal of which was the Bay of San Francisco, which a few months later he was to discover. Here he vastly increased the toil of his journey by his choice of route. He skirted the ocean until he reached the present northern boundary of the county where he encountered insurmountable barriers and was compelled to turn inland and force a perilous passage over precipitous and broken country. But we do not learn that Portola's trail was ever taken again.

In the century that followed the passage of Portola, the procession along the Camino Real was an interesting and picturesque one, changing character with the different eras. It epitomized the history of the country. Franciscan Fathers, the pioneer missionaries; Spanish couriers, gaily accoutered horsemen, swiftly journeying between Monterey and La Paz; the padres traveling from Mission to Mission; bands of cattle; Indian herders and Spanish soldiers; Royal officers and officials; Mexican and Californian cavalry; mail carriers; brigands; American soldiery and immigrant wagons and at last the Concord stage. Something of the history of the county could be learned as well from the evolution of the road. The original trail was hardly a fixed quantity. It wandered about as the exigencies of the season demanded. It might even divide itself and offer the traveller a choice of evils. Only in comparatively recent times has it acquired a definite location and the shape and style of a modern road. Today it is the perfected work of skilled engineers, a delight to all who travel over it. How that was accomplished is a story of itself and one worth recording.

Until within the last decade, roadbuilding in California was quite generally a purely local problem. Each county was divided into small road districts and each district was entitled to have expended within its boundaries whatever monies had been raised therein by taxation, and was applicable to the purpose. These amounts varied widely, and naturally where most expenditure was necessary, where the streams were widest and the country the roughest, there the assessable values were least. That was remedied to some extent by raids on other funds. A greater difficulty in the "good roads" problem was that the supervisors and road overseers to whom was entrusted the expenditure of the funds, were not always skilled engineers. A further complication arose from the fact that the labor was commonly supplied by the ranchers in the district, some of whom while clamoring for the opportunity to "work out their road tax" might not be over amenable to discipline or endowed with an overstrained sense of duty. And then too whenever a handful of settlers made their homes in some new and therefore inaccessible part of the road district, they became persistent in demanding a county road, adding still further to the financial strain. After all, much good and conscientious work must have been done even under such untoward conditions for out of the thousand and more miles of roads traversing the county, none are impassable, and many are at most seasons of the year excellent as country roads. The perfected road is a matter of the last few years. Following the example of many of the Eastern States, the proposition was presented in 1905 to the State Legislature to issue bonds to the amount of eighteen millions of dollars, the proceeds to be expended by a commission of competent engineers in the construction of a system of highways to the extent, it was estimated of about 2,500 miles. One trunk line was to run from the northern to the southern boundary of the state along the coast and a parallel one through the San Joaquin Valley. It was a new and radical departure but it appealed to the good sense of the people and, submitted to them, the proposition carried by a considerable majority. The State Highway Commission was appointed and prosecuted its work so much to the popular satisfaction that the Legislature authorized the further issuance of fifteen millions of bonds, which it was estimated would complete the system and an additional issue of three millions for the construction of certain laterals, one of which is to connect the Highway in this county with the main line in San Joaquin County and this action of the Legislature was confirmed by the people in the election of 1916 by a largely increased majority.

When the project of the State Highway was first mooted, it had been roughly estimated that, making reasonable allowance for grafters, political pets and slackers who usually fasten aand fatten on public work, the liberality expected by material men and others in dealing with public officials and the obstacles that might be interposed by grasping communities and individuals, at least fifty millions would be expended in completing the system. That the work should be completed, in a thoroughly satisfactory manner and in so short a time and for perhaps half the expected outlay is a splendid testimonial to the great executive ability and untiring energy of the commissioners. And in considering the magnitude of the achievement, it should be noted that added to the physical difficulties and engineering problems, which were at times appalling, there were other obstacles and impediments to be encountered. As constituted by statute, the commissioners were given practically unlimited discretion as to the location and as to the construction of the roads to be built. Where a road should run to best serve the public interests was rather a civic than an engineering question but it was confided to them for solution. To secure the assistance of the county officials who were often hostile to the whole project, was rather in the realms of diplomacy but it was essential. Rights of way had to be secured, county roads made part of the Highway and their courses and location changed. Bridges had to be built by the counties and of a standard required by the state. There was an apparently hopeless deadlock at the start financially. The bonds to be issued had to be sold at par and paid only four per cent. They were not saleable at the time in the market. The commissioners induced the county authorities, banks, private capitalists and landowners to purchase the bonds. In the actual construction the commissioners, in the interests of economy, let contracts for the labor only, they themselves supplying the material, the cement, oil, crushed granite, etc., and its transportation. Buying and shipping in such immense quantities

44

made a vast difference in the cost of the material. And in the execution of the work, surprised and incredulous contractors encountered inspectors who were vigilant, competent and unapproachable. In other words, the Highway Commission executed its functions as if it were a bureau of some great railroad or industrial corporation where the highest degree of efficiency was expected as a matter of course, instead of a public office, the usual field for political graft. A contemporaneous and powerful influence in this exemplification of the gospel of "Good Roads," was the evolution of the automobile. At the time the State Highway Commission was established, the machine was the costly and uncertain toy of the wealthy. In the last decade it has become the essential tool of the toiler and more especially of the farmer. Good roads are the necessary complement of the auto. The bountiful rains of California make dirt roads impassable for the time being, but on the concrete highways the teamster journeys on regardless of torrential storms. The work of the commission received added endorsement because of an enlightened self-interest which had worked a wide-spread conversion to the Good Roads movement.

Among other activities of the Highway Commission is the employment on the highways of convict labor. This aspect of its work, it is true, is hardly germane to the history of this county except for the fact that two of the gangs of convict workers are under the direction of citizens of this county, guards of the San Quentin Penitentiary, but even the scantiest summary of the work of the commission, of such manifest importance to this section, must necessarily touch this phase of it. While the immediate objective of the commission and of the people of the state in financing the project, is the construction of great trunk lines, it is the confidant expectation that ultimately, either by the initative of the several counties or of the individual road districts, no part of the state, however remote, should be inaccessible, uninhabited or valueless for lack of highways. In those sections where neither the poverty of the population nor the physical conditions made it impracticable, the influence of the achievements of the commission has been most effective. The average farmer, in California at least, whatever malicious cartoonists or feeble joke-smiths may insinuate, is highly intelligent. He is quite alive to the value of good roads but he is also capable of calculating his chances of profit if too large a part of his capital is invested in transportation facilities. Under wasteful conditions he might easily become ruinously over-capitalized. The Highway Commission has demonstrated for his benefit what the cost of construction and of upkeep of a road should be that would approximate the cost per ton of hauling on a railroad. The immediate result has been the rapid construction of laterals at local cost, rivalling in extent and character the state roads themselves. But there are other sections where the natural obstacles are too formidable to be overcome except by state aid which it would not profit the state to furnish. Here arose the opportunity to settle in some measure, the vexed question of convict labor. In the penitentiaries of the state are some four thousand men, most of them young and stalwart, fed, clothed and sheltered at the expense of the tax-payer. The latter-day conception is clear that to be so maintained in idleness or in hopeless treadmill toil only develops the criminal tendencies of the prisoner. To employ him productively excites the criticism that the work belongs to the feeble unemployed who for lack of labor may fall into evil ways. But to employ him in the construction of mountain lateral roads of such a character and in such places that otherwise they could not be built at all, is open to no such criticism. The state invests only the labor of the convict already forfeited to it and supplies his physical wants, and by way of encouragement to faithful labor, remits one day of imprisonment for every two days of good work. In return the convict building such roads takes work from no man but does work that otherwise would not be done, makes available acres for the landless that otherwise would not be opened, and stirs up counties to local road improvement that vastly increases the sum total of road work open to the free road builder. So far the cost of the roads built by convict labor has been about twenty-five per cent of its estimated cost with free labor. "The humanitarian side of the work is self-evident. The men are immeasurably better physically, which means mentally and morally. Constructive work instead of the jute mill, under blue skies and amid the beauties of mountain California instead of behind stone walls, co-operating with the State instead of being outcasts of the State, these things are alone worth the doing." I quote from the Highway Bulletin, being quite thoroughly in agreement with the ideas advanced.

The State Highways have also ended the regime of the wooden bridge, that perpetual opportunity to loot the local treasury by foreign marauders. Anybody of course could build a road or even construct a wooden culvert and determine its proper location but when it came to building a bridge and particularly to executing the preliminary drawings, the plans and elevations, specifications and calculations, it was generally understood that that was a job for a regular "bridge company." Judging from the quite uniform result, the local

46

authorities were over modest. They could hardly have done worse than did the migratory professionals. The county bridges as a rule were unskillfully and ignorantly constructed and in a few years were invariably "condemned," torn out and replaced by new ones of the same character. The standard bridges of steel or concrete of the Highway Commission were a revelation. Today, even on the county byways, the reinforced concrete bridge and culvert have become imperative and the perpetual contract letting for renewals and replacements of cheap and temporary bridges is a thing of the past.

Indeed, the by-ways, at least in the vicinity of the larger centers of population, are hardly less important than the main roads. In them the last vestige of the "post-road" survives. The postal car and the Pullman have usurped the functions of the mail coach for long journeys and distant deliveries but the postman on the rural delivery routes remains to break the monotony of farm life, bringing the news journal of the day with its record of the day's happenings in the whole world, bringing letters and packages from the ends of the earth, annihilating distance and isolation. A striking contrast to this service is the wail of Hermanagildo Sal, the comandante of San Francisco, who in 1799, writing to a friend lamented that there were no combs in the county and said despairingly, "I have no hope of receiving any for three years." Even in 1853, conditions were somewhat difficult. A notable citizen of the county at that early time wrote: "I was landed upon the beach from the boat of the steamer Sea Bird, I and another person being the only passengers on the steamer's fortnightly trip. The purser handed me the great United States mail, which I had no difficulty in concealing in my pocket." Postal facilities came in due course and the county is today as well served as any other portion of the Republic.

Good roads and railroads render travel and transportation by the ocean of lessened importance but as will be seen it is still vitally necessary and the harbors of San Luis Obispo are a highly prized asset. Up to a comparatively recent period, the imports and exports of the county were exclusively by water. Facilities were not of the best. South of the Bay of San Luis Obispo, the shore line sweeps in a great arc for a score of miles, justly regarded as the finest beach on the coast of the state but unapproachable for vessels. North of the bay are indentations at Cayucos, Morro and San Simeon, where coasting vessels have docked regularly at most seasons of the year and afforded adequate freighting facilities for the producers in the vicinity. The Bay of San Luis Obispo however had greater promise. It was of sufficient magnitude to harbor a considerable fleet of deep sea vessels and with adequate depth of water for them and good holding ground. It lacked perfect protection from the south only and there a breakwater was necessary. That was finally constructed by the Government and now great "oil-tankers," the largest of their class are constantly loading at the wharves in the harbor and carrying the products of the wells of the San Joaquin Valley and of those nearer at hand, to all parts of the world. If one had space and time, it would interest the present writer if not the reader to recall the efforts, extending over a score of years, which were persistently made by public-spirited citizens, to secure this improvement to the harbor. Our representatives in Congress were never lukewarm but San Luis Obispo was a small spot on the map of

MORRO ROCK

an inconsiderable state. The commercial necessity of the harbor was problematical. It was a problem for the future. The stronger immediate argument in its favor was its usefulness as a port of refuge, the only one possible in two hundred miles of forbidding coast line and that was made emphatic by the plight of the "Queen," a large coasting steamer, crowded with passengers, which sprung a leak far out at sea opposite the port and barely reached it in a sinking condition. Appropriations were finally made by Congress amounting to some $300,000 and a breakwater constructed, chiefly of massive stone lightered from Morro Rock. The harbor has now a number of wharves, one built by the county in a public-spirited

48

mood, the more important and earliest one being that operated by the Pacific Coast Railway.

The railway wharf is really a monument to local enterprise. It too was a product of the early seventies. Prior to its construction vessels had landed their passengers and merchandise on the inner or eastern side of the bay at first by boats upon the beach or derricks from the shore and later by wharves extending out a short distance to a limited depth of water. But as that was before the day of the breakwater, landing during the winter months was often dangerous and impracticable, so much so, that ultimately the heavy seas broke up and washed away the wharves and landing places. With greater wisdom, the railway wharf was located by its builders on the farther side of the bay along the promontory extending southward and where it would be protected in great measure from the southeasters of winter. It extended out to a depth of water amply sufficient for the coasting steamers of the day and around the rocky and precipitous bay shore to Avila, a tramway was constructed as being more practicable than a wagon road. Considering the local conditions, the scanty population and the scarcity of capital, the building of the wharf was a very considerable achievement. Happily it justified the expectations of its builders, was profitable in itself and speedily led to further and more important development.

CHAPTER VII

GROWTH AND DEVELOPMENT

Considering the history of the county during the seventy years of its existence, it would seem that the "70's" were its most important years, its years of greatest initiative and progress. In those years systematic roadbuilding was begun; the sea-ports utilized; railroads constructed; many of the great ranchos divided and sold to settlers; the public school system organized; the county seat incorporated and the population of the county quadrupled. Those were the years immediately following the close of the Civil war and resulting conditions in the Eastern States doubtless induced immigration into California from which this county benefited to some extent. But whatever may have been the cause, during the period in question, this section seemed a special center of attraction. About the beginning of the decade, several hundreds were added to the population of the town. They came from all points of the compass, ex-Confederates from the South and ex-Union men from the North and West, many from other parts of California. They were for the most part strangers to each other but all, with curious unanimity, inspired with the common conviction that Fortune would surely smile upon them; that the county promised rapid growth; that the climate was perfect and the country a Garden of Eden. Most of them were men of mature years and ripened judgment. All the professions and all lines of business were represented among them and while none of them were wealthy, none were without means sufficient for their business requirements. They were men of vision and enterprise, high qualities that were assuredly needed to cope with the local conditions. Aside from climate, soil and scenery, these were not alluring. There was an ill-built Mexican village, without streets or sidewalks, sewers or water, fire protection or street lights. It was bisected by a winding stream which it was not always possible to ford. This village was set down in the midst of a vast territory, full of possibilities for the future but closed to immediate settlement and barren of resource. Most of the Spanish grants were still intact, their owners still pursuing contentedly the pastoral existence to which they were accustomed. The county still remained almost as isolated, as difficult of access as in its colonial days. By land a strenuous journey of several days in a "mud wagon" had to be endured to reach the county either from the north or south. Travellers preferred the route by sea although the conditions there were primitive.

However the new population of that time, whose numbers slowly but steadily increased, were in no wise discouraged. They were for the most part Americans, not unfamiliar with pioneer conditions and constructive work, the creation of civic life, the formative processes of a new civil existence appealed to them. It was rather a joyous time, one certainly full of interest. The rich future of the country was in its agricultural resources. To encourage their development, transportation of the crops to distant markets was essential which meant the improvement of the harbor. The initial effort as stated was the construction of the "railroad" wharf. That afforded safe and commodious landing for the coasting vessels and, extended and improved, is still the important one. But the harbor was eight miles distant from the town and our enterprising citizens at once planned the construction of a "railroad" to the port. It was an ambitious project to be undertaken by a community practically without spare capital but the road was bravely started and several miles actually constructed. Then the promoters secured the co-operation of outside capitalists and the road was completed to the county seat and in due process of time extended to Arroyo Grande and then to Santa Maria in the adjoining county and then to Los Alamos and to Los Olivos. The transportation problem was solved for many years. The Pacific Coast Railway, which was the final designation of the "San Luis Obispo Railroad" and the "San Luis Obispo and Santa Maria Valley Railroad," became an important feeder and adjunct to the coast steamer lines and large passenger and freight vessels made regular and frequent landings at the port and furnished ample and excellent service.

As had been confidently anticipated by the promoters, this achievement contributed largely to the prompt development of this section. Further progress followed the change of ownership of many of the large ranchos. In bestowing upon the grantees, these tracts of ten or twenty or more thousands of acres, the Mexican authorities, it would seem, often acted with little discrimination. Frequently the beneficiaries were able to make but limited use of their holdings. Little experienced in business affairs, lacking perhaps in energy and enterprise, they were often victimized by the unscrupulous, created

51

debts that they could have no means of paying and lost their estates piece-meal. And there were others of the same order of intelligence who were unable to forecast the future value of their land, readily found purchasers at their own estimate of its worth and lost a fortune. So the era of subdivision and settlement began. Surveyors' stakes dotted the wide expanse, prospective buyers were driven about in all directions and plentifully supplied with lithographed maps and boom literature. The aspect of the country changed rapidly. Fenced fields appeared, great barns and windmills, fine stock and horses, fields of grain, the gang plow and the threshing machine. And while profitably exercising their several callings and incidentally laboring for the general development of the country, the pioneers of the new era were intent as well on the needs of the future city. A first step was to secure the ownership of the town lots to their claimants or occupants. The real title was still in the United States acquired by treaty from Mexico. The possessors were mere trespassers. The matter was laid before Congress and remedied by the passage of an Act which granted the town lots to the city for the benefit of the actual occupants within a certain area. The lands so granted were surveyed and deeds executed giving title by metes and bounds. The larger part of the townsite was the level "Priests' Gardens" but it was cut off by the Arroyo which meandered lazily along in the rainless months but in the wet season was often an unfordable torrent and so at each cross street had to be bridged. That accomplished, many quite fine residences were erected in the new section, new business quarters established and the City Hall built there. Water of course was a prime necessity and among the earliest steps taken in constructing the new city was the formation of a company of local capitalists for supplying it. For many years the Company fairly met the needs of the community. In the ten years from 1870 to 1880, the crude Mexican village became a fairly representative American town. Many private residences, schools, churches, halls and business blocks had been erected, much public work done on the streets and elsewhere, an expensive Court House built and the population had grown from 600 to 2,500.

This growth and progress was perhaps not phenomenal. Peculiar conditions favored it. Nevertheless that so much was accomplished within the limited time was unquestionably due to the energy and initiative of the few scores of rather unusual men who chanced as it would seem at about the same period, to entertain identical views as to the future of this section. They were materially aided in their efforts by other considerable and notable accessions which were made

52

to the population of the county during the epochal '70s or about that time from the several countries of Europe. The most in evidence perhaps was the colony from Switzerland, chiefly from the Canton Ticino. It is said that the emigration to California largely depleted the population of that Canton, to its great damage. Just how the hegira started is a problem but one not difficult of solution. Way back in 1849, the days of gold, adventurous spirits in Ticino had responded to the call from the far distant land of fortune and if their dreams of sudden wealth in gold-hunting had not been realized they at least found golden opportunities in other directions and their success induced many of their friends and relatives to follow in their footsteps. The stream of immigration was slow but constant and persists to this day. While the Swiss followed every occupation, dairying was the favorite one and this and other coast counties was specially sought by them as being specially adapted to that business. From Marin to Santa Barbara, along the ocean the Swiss dairymen predominate. In these latter days when labor-saving seems the last word in civilization, particularly to the individual seeking to avoid exertion and hunting the "easiest way," the tale of the Swiss immigrant should be inspiring. Perhaps in leaving his native land, there was not that sense of heart-sick exile that we have learned to associate with the native of the Emerald Isle, driven by bitter need to leave his wretched home. But still, Switzer and Irishman alike have a just and abiding pride in the brilliant history of their respective countries, in the resplendent names which adorn them, a deep and abiding love for their mother land and admiration for their excelling beauties. But there are differences in their lamentations. The young Swiss parted from home and family with no sense of compulsion or escape from tyrannical surroundings but with a sense of joyous adventure, with boundless confidence in a future bright with hope for himself and ultimately for the loved ones he left behind him. The biographies of our Swiss-Americans, immigrants in those earlier days are curiously similar and betray an identity of origin and environment which fitted them admirably for the pioneer conditions they were to meet. Most of them came from forbears that they would now consider desperately poor. They were sheltered in rude cottages, suffered actual privation at times and secured the very necessaries of existence by the hardest toil. But that did not daunt those earnest souls. They reared large families and gave them stalwart frames, habits of industry and integrity and fair education. Reaching the age of seventeen or eighteen, by hook or crook, by painful economies or loans perhaps to the point of bankruptcy, our future citizen was launched forth with the slenderest provision, on the long voyage to California. Usually he found his way to the ranch of some relative who knew the breed and was glad to have so sturdy and capable a hand, however unskilled. Perhaps the pay was small for a while but not for long. The young recruit speedily learned his value. Said one of them to me: "I got $18 a month on a ranch in Marin County the first year after I came but after eight years I knew the business thoroughly and I had saved enough from my wages to make the first payments on a ranch in this county, a fine piece of land of about 400 acres. After that it was simply a question of work. Work? I worked eighteen hours a day and in every hour I did twice as much as any man I could hire." Endowed with such physical and mental ability, with such determination to succeed, of course "fortune" has favored him. He married early one of his young countrywomen, and now advanced in years, an honored grandfather, he has a considerable fortune, has occupied public positions of importance and is a highly considered citizen and a very thorough American. And that is the story of most of the Swiss immigrants. Diligent, shrewd and saving, they speedily become independent, marry early, have no false notions of race suicide, fill the public schools, quickly acquire an adequate knowledge of English, became naturalized, are active and intelligent politically and —before the present war—occasionally journeyed to the mother country to visit and help the surviving relatives, perhaps as poverty-stricken as of old except for such assistance, but rarely if ever with any idea of remaining there, or abandoning this country of their adoption. A strong breed that has helped materially in making the history of the county.

Almost as numerous as the Swiss and having many of the same characteristics of thrift and industry are the Portuguese, coming chiefly from the Azore Islands. In the straitened conditions in which they were born in their native islands, in their early difficulties in faring forth to seek more hopeful opportunity in a far distant country, in their strenuous efforts to accumulate and in the success which they have quite generally realized, Portuguese and Swiss are alike. Whether the same untiring exertion is to be anticipated from their immediate descendants is a matter of doubt. The rising generation has known nothing of the hard conditions that made their fathers grasp opportunity with such determination and like the scions of the older strains in the county they may be expected to seek what they may regard as less arduous careers.

Without exception, I think, all the other European countries have added liberally but to a lesser degree to our population, but however cosmopolitan in origin, the climate, environment and equality of condition have done their work. In the third generation, the racial characteristics of Swede, Portuguese and the man from Texas are hardly distinguishable.

The later years of the nineteenth century added nothing spectacular to the history of the county. It was a time of slow but continuous development, the subdivision of many of the large ranchos and the sale of the smaller tracts so created to new settlers. But in those and succeeding years, continual efforts were being made to hasten the construction of the Southern Pacific Railway along the coast, something which had been hoped for if not expected for many years.

As a matter of fact a principal moving cause of that unanimity of purpose exhibited by the immigrants to the county in the '70s, was the quite general conviction that it would be but a short time, a few years at most before the completion of the road between San Francisco and Los Angeles, a consummation assuring tthe happiest effects upon the fortunes of the populations along the line. Everything seemed to justify that conviction. In 1870, the San Francisco and San Jose Railroad having been extended to Gilroy, passed into the hands of the enterprising gentlemen who had won great fame and fortunes in completing the Central Pacific Railroad. They were wizards of finance. Starting absolutely without money or credit, they had under the most difficult conditions, succeeded not only in carrying through a world-famous enterprise which had cost untold millions but also, incidentally diverting quite a number of those millions into their own pockets. In their hands the utmost confidence was felt that the road would be finished quite speedily. The road became the Southern Pacific Railway and under its new management continued vigorously the work of further construction. In 1874 it had reached Soledad, 143 miles from San Francisco. Another 100 miles would bring the road to the City of San Luis Obispo. But then construction ceased, not to be resumed for thirteen years. Those were not days like the present, in which business men think in billions. Figures of that size were related to national debts or the resources of a whole country. The close corporations of the Central and Southern Pacific Railways had their difficulties in financing their ambitious projects which merely required millions. The project of the Coast road became a side issue with them. It was safe in their hands. It could wait. It controlled already all the traffic of the coast region without need of further immediate construction. And they had more important use for all the funds they could command in building their road through the San Joaquin Valley and to Los Angeles. So, for those many years, our pioneers waited with hopes deferred but not extinguished, and at last in 1881, they had the satisfaction of learning that construction had been resumed. The work progressed steadily and in 1889 it reached Santa Margarita, 236½ miles from San Francisco and about ten miles from San Luis Obispo. There it encountered the first great physical obstacle. To go further it must cross the Santa Lucia range, a tremendous and costly engineering feat. Further progress, it was understood was not immediately contemplated. In the meantime the Southern Pacific had built north from Los Angeles along the coast to Ellwood in Santa Barbara County, leaving untouched a "gap" of 120 miles. Without doubt the railroad company intended ultimately to complete the road. It was essential to their system. Dependent upon local traffic, without through business and in competition with ocean transportation, the large investment already made was comparatively unprofitable. But as may be imagined the people of the western part of the county and more especially the townsfolk of San Luis Obispo, many of whom had watchfully waited for fifteen or twenty years for the culmination of their hopes, viewed with impatience and disgust this apparent final abandonment of construction. Instead of benefiting them, the railroad so far had been a serious detriment. It had taken from them the business of the eastern part of the county, built up rival towns, materially reduced their population and lessened their values. Much indignation was manifested and many meetings held. There was a convention held at San Jose, attended by delegates from all the coast counties at which there was much discussion and energetic resolutions adopted. Finally at a mass meeting in San Luis Obispo, in April, 1889, Mr. C. P. Huntington appeared by invitation and presented his ultimatum. In the right of way from Santa Margarita to the southern county line should be procured and given to the Southern Pacific Railway Company, work would be resumed and in due time the "gap" closed. Mr. Huntington was an able financier and was noted for his frugality. No chance for a profitable dicker ever escaped him whether for his personal benefit or for the corporate interests he might represent. The survey for the railroad skirted the city, cutting through a great number of small residence lots. To find their owners, many of them non-resident, to trace their titles, to agree upon a purchase price, more than all, to pay the price, would involve a considerable sacrifice of time and money. Let San Luis Obispo do it. And San Luis Obispo did. It was a rather singular arrangement, a mere verbal agreement not between the two corporations interested but between Huntington, the railroad magnate and the people at large. The people in accepting the situation gathered voluntarily, organized in simple fashion, appointed committees and apportioned the work and after three years or more of persistent effort, the last deeds were delivered to the railroad company. It had cost the citizens about fifty thousand dollars, raised by a scheme of apportionment. A percentage of the assessed value of all the property within the city limits was assumed as requisite and the several owners were invited to pay their pro rata respectively and the great majority did so. A numerous committee was appointed to urge this co-operation and the members went by twos and speedily and effectively covered the small districts assigned them. The whole undertaking bristled with difficulties and the satisfactory completion of the task was a matter of general rejoicing. Doubtless Mr. Huntington was pleased also. He had effected a considerable saving for himself and partners, probably several times the cost to the city. He was true to his word at all events. In October, 1892, the crossing of the Santa Lucia range was started. In May, 1894, the road was finished to Sàn Luis Obispo and on the 31st of May, 1901, the gap was closed. It was in October, 1860, that construction of the road was commenced at San Francisco. Over forty years it had taken to complete it to Los Angeles. It had been the sport of circumstance. At one time, the managers of the road determined to change the route at Gilroy going thence eastward to the San Joaquin Valley instead of southward. Again when the road reached San Miguel, it was understood that from there the road would be diverted eastward to the San Joaquin Valley. And that extension as a lateral, it has been supposed would ultimately form part of the Southern Pacific system. Indeed about the time of his celebrated meeting with the populace of San Luis Obsipo in 1889, Mr. Huntington said to the writer, answering the suggestion that probably an east and west road would be more valuable to our city than the completion of the coast road; "the chances are you will see the road from San Miguel to the San Joaquin Valley built first?" an enigmatical assertion that seemed to afford doubtful assurance of any immediate construction in either direction.

There have been many regrets expressed that an "East and West" railroad has not materialized. The project of giving the vast empire of the San Joaquin Valley direct connection with the sea at San Luis Obispo Bay by a hundred miles of road, easily and cheaply constructed, has been an alluring one and may some day be realized. But there has arisen a formidable rival to the railroad in the concrete highway and the automobile and auto truck. Like the trolley in other parts of the country, it may be an effective competitor. The Camino Real, paralleling the Coast road throughout its extent, is dotted with autos that require incessant activity on the part of the "speed cops" to moderate their swift flight and the lateral of the State Highway from San Luis Obispo now assured by the vote of the people at the recent election, will provide an east and west road that for so short a haul for passengers and freight may render the construction of a railroad unnecessary and inadvisable.

CHAPTER VIII

FLOCKS AND HERDS

Something over fifty years ago, one of that number of enterprising gentlemen, to whom allusion has been made as "the pioneers of the '70s," and who was later a prominent leader among them, after a first quite thorough exploration of the county, tersely expressed his conclusions in the phrase, "It is *cow heaven.*" As from long and intimate acquaintance with "sis cow," (as a distinguished author usually styled the animal) the judgment of the enthusiastic stockraiser would have been taken as final without calling for evidence. Nevertheless, at the time in question, the bovine Elysium was comparatively untenanted. Stockraising had experienced strange vicissitudes. In 1772, the amazed aborigines had beheld driven to the site of the future Mission of San Luis Obispo, the "21 bulls, 9 cows and 8 calves," the spoil of the abandoned missions of Baja, California, which was the meagre allotment to each of the foundations of Padre Serra in this great field. After the intemperate conditions of their breeding place, after the long, exhausting drive over barren deserts, gaunt with hunger and thirst, one can imagine that their characterization of their new habitat, expressed in their own fashion, would be practically that of their friend so many years later. It was, and is, a land specially adapted to their needs. The dense foliage of the wide-spreading live oaks and cottonwoods afforded all necessary shelter from the hottest noonday of the rainless season or the fiercest gales of so-called winter. With the first rains, with magic swiftness, the level valleys, the rolling hills, the deep canyons and the far distant slopes of the low mountains, clear to their summits, were covered with the rich native grasses, growing lush and luxuriant until long after the cessations of the rains. And then during all the sunny months the ripened indigenous grains, alfilaria, wild oats and clover afforded ample provender until the heavens should again be opened and the rains descend. And always, at short distances, seeking their winding, "easiest way," from the Santa Lucias to the ocean were arroyos, turbulent streams in the days of torrential rains, dwindling during the rainless months, at times disappearing under their nominal beds and then reappearing in pools in sheltered and shady spots. Under such favoring conditions, the little band of cattle at the Mission increased and multiplied with wonderful rapidity. Perhaps there were later importations. Horses, sheep and goats were added to the menagerie. In a few years the numbers of the animals could only be estimated. A few calves wandering from maternal protection might fall a victim to the prowling coyote or mountain lion and a limited number of young cattle be slaughtered for the necessities of the small human population, but these demands made no sensible inroad on the vast and constantly increasing herds. There was no market available. Commerce was practically prohibited in the colonial days and the occasional "drogher," touching surreptitiously at the port was the only customer for the small accumulations of hides and horns and tallow. Conditions changed somewhat under Mexican rule but it was not until the discovery of gold and the larger American occupation that stockraising became a profitable industry. Then began the continuous procession of the herds to the northern markets and an era of sudden wealth for the ranchowners that rivalled that of the luckiest of the gold diggers. Like most swift and unexpected fortune, it bred in them a spirit of wild extravagance that not infrequently ended in disaster. For again the conditions changed. The great immigration and the resulting splendid market brought cattle by the thousand from the Mississippi states and Texas. Other sections of California, particularly the coast counties in the vicinity of San Francisco, seized the opportunity and engaged extensively in the business of stockraising as an easy road to fortune. Then the price of cattle rapidly diminished but only with the effect of clearing the way for the skilled dairyman, the elimination of the wild native cattle and the breeding of better and more profitable strains. These causes however had but little to do with the disappearance referred to of the cattle of the county. It chanced that at this juncture, it was in 1864, there came a season of drought, the only one of like severity of which Dame Nature has been guilty in this section since the days of Padre Serra. Of course it had not been anticipated, no provision had been made for it, there was no refuge within driving distance for the poor animals and all but a small remnant perished.

This great disaster had far reaching results. At that time stockraising was the chief if not the only productive industry in the county. It was still largely in the hands of the grantees from the Mexican government, more adapted to a carefree existence and the exercise of a boundless hospitality than to the hardships of a business career. Fine saddle horses, elegant and costly equipment, fine dress, sumptuous entertainment, more than all, "a cigarito and a talk" made their happiness. Their countless herds were their bank and their capital. Their broad acres were an incident, essential of course but valueless to them intrinsically. Unable to restock their ranchos, without means longer to pay the taxes assessed upon them, pressed by creditors and facing ruin, purchasers at any price for their holdings were welcomed. So with the elimination of the Spanish cow began the elimination of the Spanish grant.

The reconstruction period in the cattle industry which followed was along very different lines. Theretofore cattle had been raised for their beef value. Milk, butter and cheese were rare articles upon the tables of the old rancheros. The gentle milch cow was an unknown animal. Under the new dispensation, there were introduced fine imported strains of Durham, Jersey and Holstein, the big ranchos were divided into manageable tracts, each one a dairy farm with an expert manager and cheese and butter maker and a skilled gang of workers. The grazing upon the ranges was supplemented by crops of grain, hay and roots. In a few years our "cow heaven" was more heavily stocked than ever. The pioneers in the dairy industry had been speedily followed by hundreds of others, most of them from Sonoma, Marin and Santa Cruz counties, men of long experience who found here unequalled opportunities for the successful prosecution of the business and for the acquisition of cheap lands admirably adapted for it. In a few years this county which had formerly not even produced dairy products sufficient for the wants of its very limited population could justly claim to be the leading county in the state in its exports of cheese and butter.

For many years dairying continued to be the prime industry of the county but in the course of time other pursuits were found to be equally lucrative and engaged the efforts of the ranchers. Success was not always a certainty. Something more than a capacity for hard work is requisite to constitute a skilled dairyman, and from the standpoint of the consumer it would seem that that is the single talent which a large proportion of cheese and butter makers possess. Some such conditions affected our dairymen it is said, and among the great number of small dairies, there were widely differing standards of excellence and variance of opinion as to salient points in the business, sanitation, treatment of diseases, cleanly methods and the like. Of late years, the making of cheese aand butter for local and distant markets, though of somewhat lessened importance, is still a major industry and State inspection and a realization of the business value of sanitary methods have resulted in radical improvement.

Silos and adequate provision for the cattle when feed becomes scanty on their limited pastures, the weeding out of cows proving unprofitable as milk producers, careful breeding, the importation of high grade stock, have had like favorable effects. The reduced production of cheese and butter on the big ranches does not imply any diminution in the extent and value of the dairy interests. Instead of these products, the cream itself is sent to market, the dairyman finding a greater profit in accepting an immediate cash return from the large creameries established at the county seat. Incidentally it results that the business is shared by many small proprietors or general farmers whose small herds would not justify the installing of a dairy outfit, however limited. The family "auto," its tonneau occupied by the tall cans is constantly met "on the road to town" and these cars rival in aggregate importance the great auto trucks, heavily laden with like receptacles, despatched from distant dairies or gathered up along the road by the trucks in their daily or still more frequent journeys. In fact it is a fair assumption, that to the invention of the automobile is largely due the latest evolution of the dairy industry. Creameries were no novelty. Years ago, when the "separator" was then a recent invention, that ingenious mechanism in conjunction with the co-operative factory, promised great things for the dairyman and a number of "creameries" were established in various parts of the county. But for various reasons they proved unsatisfactory and one after the other closed down. Perhaps nothing could have been devised that would have excited the ire and disgust of the rancher to a greater degree than the automobile. He had scented an enemy in the bicycle which had threatened the usefulness of the horse and the consumption and consequent price of hay. But that disturber of his peace of mind had proved a false alarm. Then the scent was multiplied variously at the apparition of the "gas wagon." A few of the first machines that were made reached this county and as they had an inveterative habit of coming to grief whenever their venturesome drivers succeeded in getting a good distance from their garage, there was some lucrative consolation and sardonic joy for the passing teamster in hitching his terrified team to the luckless auto and dragging it home. But after a few years the stalled auto was a rare spectacle. Alert "demonstrators" were able to show the most stubborn Missourians the economy in time and money resulting from their employment until now the machine is regarded as the essential part of the equipment of every well regulated farm. Unlike the farm horses, it needs no Sunday lay-off and the day of rest is brightened to the lonesome country home by cheerful excursions in the "car."

But in spite of the automobile and its near relation the farm motor, also very generally in use, there would seem to be no diminution in the number or value of the horses of the county. For certain exigencies of farm life, it would seem that the horse is still essential. Oxen and mules have been rarely used since the American conquest and only to a limited extent before that. The pack mule was an inheritance from old Spain, and oxen were essential to drag the clumsy carreta and both vanished when better freight carriers were found, but without the horse the history of the county might have read very differently. Swift transportation has transformed the conditions of the whole world in the last century. It was the horse that conquered the magnificent distances of California for the Spaniard; that made possible the speedy communication between its remote settlements, without which it would have been only a succession of isolated and unprotected hamlets instead of a comparatively compact colony. The horse was a chief factor in the existence of State and individual. Without the vaquero there could have been no limitless herds of cattle; without the mounted soldier, the herding of the natives would doubtless have proved impracticable on any large scale. Without the gaily caparisoned steed much of the light of life and romance of the land would have been lost. Perhaps if the horse had finished his evolution from his faraway six-toed ancestor, here on this continent where it began instead of in Europe, the Californian Indian might have benefited thereby and have mounted higher in the scale of humanity. The mounted Apache was a more formidable foe to the trained cavalryman than was the Pequot to the Puritan.

But while the conquistadores were so greatly indebted to the equine race, the candid writer will question whether the obligation was fittingly recognized. At the time of the American occupation, there were horses without number in the country but fine animals of the race were rare exceptions. The average "mustang" was a singular combination of good and evil qualities, the latter largely predominating. He became partially domesticated like any other wild animal, through fear. Perhaps kindness might have been as effective if it had ever been tried but in those early days and perhaps during the preceding centuries which followed the discovery of the new world, the S. P. C. A. had not been invented. There was an unending conflict between the cruelty and brutality of man and the viciousness he fostered. Nothing more perfect was ever organized. As instruments of torture for the four-legged brute, the Spanish bit, powerful enough to break the animal's jaw and the Spanish spur with its murderous spikes, could not be surpassed. And in reprisal, the ferocious efforts of the otherwise helpless mustang to unseat his rider and to escape being broken were truly admirable. Of course the unequal struggle could only result in a cowed and broken-spirited beast, still vicious but submissive. But in spite of his inherited just resentment at his treatment by the humans, his instinctive revolt at ill usage, his dwarfed size and mean disposition, certain redeeming qualities were always conceded to him. He was as sure-footed upon the rough mountain trails as a goat. He could rival that animal in finding sustenance. He was swift and tireless and on long journeys displayed marvelous endurance. And after all the last named attribute included all the others and explained them. It was commonly claimed to account for his excellencies that he was of the race of the Spanish barb, supposedly sprung from Arabian stock. That might be true in some instances but could hardly have a general application. The more plausible theory is that the progenitors of the mustang might as well have been the Rosinantes and crowbaits of old Spain; that it was rather the Darwinian "survival of the fittest" which is responsible for that wonderful endurance demanded by the struggle for existence. It was no part of the regimen of their owners that food should be provided for them and if in scouting for sustenance in far distant wilds, there were wild beasts to encounter only the fleet and surefooted escaped. Left to his own resources, to wander at will, the mustang would have reached the equine perfection which Nature intended. The wild horse of the plains demonstrated that. But man's inhumanity and maltreatment balked Nature and left the lower animal only the endurance which enabled him to survive. When the "gringos" came, they brought with them horses of a different character and race. Most of them also had passed through hard experiences. The long journey across the plains, the suffering and privation endured in traversing the trackless wastes of the deserts and struggling over endless mountain ranges had weeded out the weaker animals. Those that survived were of special value to the country for that reason. And as draught animals were in great request in those early days when the lure of the newly discovered gold brought in the multitudes, there were large importations of high grade horses from the Eastern States and from Europe. Trusted agents were despatched to England and France for long-pedigreed Clydesdales and Percherons. And in those days of sudden wealth, as might be expected, the "sport of kings" was not neglected. Horse-racing had always been a favorite amusement with the native Californians and to the Americans from the Western and Southern States more especially, the love of the race-track and the fleet courser was traditional. So, many of the kings and queens of the turf were brought out to the coast and race meets in different parts of the state were many and were largely attended and records were made and much money changed hands. Incidentally there was the good result, that the breeding of horses became an extensive industry and the stock of the country was greatly and generally improved. In this county the business became quite important. To some extent it had always been so. From the colonial times, the county had been noted for its fine horses, either because the clement climate and easy conditions had made the inhabitants more considerate in the treatment of their beasts or because the animals responded to their better environment or perhaps the ranchers of the county took special pride in their fine stock. When Fremont granted the boon of life to Jose Pico, the captive of his bow and spear, on the memorable occasion of the siege and surrender of the city of San Luis Obispo, the Mexican magnate gratefully bestowed on the American General his choicest possessions, two superb horses, and demonstrated their splendid qualities in that continuous round trip from Los Angeles to Monterey and return, previously mentioned. As in other parts of the state in its early days, the race-track was an essential factor in breeding for speed and for many years the annual "meet" was our chief fashionable event. Many of the wealthier ranchers took great pride in their roadsters and not infrequently had some high-pedigreed youngster in training at the track for the coming races. San Luis Obispo County was made one of the districts of the State Agricultural Association when that institution was created by the Legislature and the proposition of an annual county fair created much enthusiasm. The fairs were held at the county seat and its citizens subscribed quite liberally to meet the necessary expense. A large pavilion was erected for the display of exhibits and a fine level tract of land, a short distance from town was purchased and laid out as a mile track and during the year the track was a busy and interesting place, its long row of stables filled with horses of more or less high degree, and during race week there were capacity crowds in attendance. Vehicles of all descriptions lined the home stretch and enthusiastic people filled grand stand and betting ring. But in the course of time the interest waned, other towns in the county claimed the privilege of holding the fair, debt and discouragement followed, and finally the "track" reverted to its original and more profitable agricultural uses in private ownership. The evils which commonly attend the race-track were largely responsible for this result, but it was also true that here, as in other parts of the state, the business of horse-raising at least for fast and fashionable stock, was largely abandoned. As a purely money-making venture it was not attractive to the hard-headed capitalist. It appealed to the pride of possession and the instincts of the "fancier," but the great breeding farms of the state, like those of Stanford or Baldwin, which produced marvelous animals that captured the speed records of the world were rather the pleasure grounds of their millionaire owners than investments for profit. The business was still less hopeful for the man of lesser means. So of later years the sober draught animal is more in evidence and the former jehu takes to the "auto," pursued by the speed-cop.

In the roll of its wealth and in various other ways, sheep have counted largely in the history of the county. In their first ministrations the padres considered wool essential. Like other missionaries to benighted colored races, the first step apprehended as essential to civilize and Christianize the native was to clothe him. Nudity was incompatible with right living. When his nakedness was disclosed to him he would be convicted of sin and vice versa. The doctrine is primeval, Edenic. So sheep in droves were brought in from Mexico, rude looms constructed and fabrics and garments produced in quantity. Ample occupation was so afforded the young female natives. Cloth came from Spain and Mexico as well and flax was raised and linen made, but there were sheep in countless numbers. Existing records casually estimate as among the possessions of the Mission of San Luis Obispo at the time of the secularization, "eight sheep farms averaging nine thousand sheep to each farm," and of "forty-seven thousand sheep" belonging to the Mission of San Miguel. Doubtless the happy Indians were completely clothed and wool entered largely into the structure of their garments. To the well-intentioned priests, the conditions doubtless appeared to be vastly improved. Perhaps the Indian saw matters from a different angle. He was the distant predecessor of the fresh-air advocate of our day. The soft well-tanned skin of the wild beast had been his garment when necessity compelled any. To be completely encased in the rough weaves of wool and linen must have been to him a foretaste of purgatory. And in like fashion, instead of the time-honored "sleeping porch" on Mother Earth, with no other covering than the star-lit sky, he was herded in a foul

66

adobe hut and properly and decently blanketed. It was mistaken kindness. The race vanished.

But large as were the flocks in the palmy days of the padres or in the flush times which came with the great gold immigration, still, in the score of years following the latter epoch, they were vastly increased. There were captains of industry in those days, quite able to observe flood tides in the affairs of men and thus be led on to fortune. Some of these chose this county and northern Santa Barbara as their theater of operations. The conjunction of favorable circumstances which appealed to them was the unlimited and growing market for mutton and wool, the gradual disappearance of the inferior native stock, the great areas of available pasture and the climatic advantages. The enterprise involved the driving of great flocks of graded sheep from Ohio and neighboring states over the thousands of miles which intervened, a most difficult and hazardous undertaking. Of the first droves, out of 6,000 sheep only one-quarter survived the perils of the road and reached the valleys of Southern California. Nevertheless there was a wide margin of profit even then. Energy and enterprise had its reward. In a few years the coterie referred to had purchased out of their gains, some 200,000 acres of the finest lands in this section and were noted as the largest sheepowners in the state. In later years this tide of fortune receded, the government lands adjacent to the grants and which had afforded free pasture were largely pre-empted, the grant lands became too valuable to be used as sheep runs and there were tariff changes which opened the door to the wools of Australia and South America.

And so in due course, sheep-raising gave place to dairying and agriculture.

CHAPTER IX

AGRICULTURE

At the present time, that would be a very modest Californian indeed who would not quite sincerely claim that his state was the granary of the world, and that if called upon to do so, it could feed all the peoples thereof. He might accept the assistance of the other Pacific States and demand adequate means of transportation by land and sea and due protection from British blockades or German submarines. But serene in his knowledge of the illimitable possibilities of his state in the production of breadstuffs, he would be incredulous as to the existence of any demand in that direction which it could not supply. And unless he was one of those ancient veterans, still lagging superfluous on the stage whose knowledge of California conditions extends to the decade "before the War," it would be difficult to convince him that for a number of years after the American occupation, it was regarded as indubitable that California was not adapted to agriculture. While the pioneers embraced all sorts and conditions of men, a large proportion doubtless were acquainted with farm life. "Back home," they knew what happened when on the growing crops in the summer time there came a drouth if of only a few weeks' duration. But here it was not weeks but months without rain. With the last showers of April the adobe soil baked to bricklike hardness and shrank and seamed and split in all directions; cracks appeared a foot deep in which you could thrust your hand, sideways, and vegetation shrivelled away and disappeared. With irrigation something might be done, where surface water could be obtained and perhaps along the rivers intensive culture might be profitable. But the valleys and plains were hopeless. Tales of the grain-raising of the missions were heard incredulously. The conditions in Southern California might be different. Still, in spite of so much oracular wisdom and the subject was a fruitful one for the newspapers of the time, experimenting went on diligently. Prices were enormous and the prizes for success were glittering. Spring and seed time and "frost out of the ground," it was discovered, came in September instead of March. After the cessation of the rains the grain fields ripened gloriously and there were even crops which demanded the long rainless months for their highest fruition. The experimental stage speedily passed and while many of the gold seekers had "made their pile" or had failed to do so and in either event had gone back to "the States" and their old associations, a new tide of immigration set in attracted by the possibilities of successful agriculture.

San Luis Obispo County did not perhaps need assurances as to its adaptability for agriculture and particularly for grain-raising although to read the careful, painstaking editorials of its newspaper as late as 1868—it had but one—it might be inferred that the matter was still open to argument. Perhaps the earnest and able efforts of that early writer were not without good effect. At all events they were timely and the next decade brought radical changes. Just about a century had passed since the first white occupation and during all that time, the same primitive methods of farming had been followed and the same absurd implements had been insisted upon. Wisdom had died with Solomon and the methods of the Syrian peasant were still infallible in the fields of the mission fathers. The land was not plowed. An upright stake with a metal point was fixed to a beam which was hauled along by oxen to whose horns the beam was fastened. There was no furrow and this scratching of the surface must have involved an enormous amount of labor. The seed was thrown broadcast in the time-honored fashion and brushed in with the branches of trees or forced in by dragging heavy logs over the ground. Sometimes there was no attempt at disturbing the soil. The seed was simply sown upon the native earth. Colton wrote that in 1827, the majordomo of the Mission of San Luis Obispo, "scattered on the ground without having first plowed it, 120 bushels of wheat and then scratched it in with things called harrows and harvested from the same over 7,000 bushels."

The agricultural conditions of the county prior to the '70s resulted from no lack of knowledge or appreciation of the possibilities on the part of the inhabitants. It was a matter of business judgment. After the secularization of the missions, the local dominion fell into the hands of the few lords of the soil, the holders of the vast grants which practically covered the most available arable lands of the county. Many of these grantees were Spanish, American or English. They had accepted a nominal fealty to the Mexican government, and in some instances at least, with equal sincerity, the Catholic faith; and had married into influential families. As the result of such alliances, it may be fairly assumed, they were endowed with lands proportionate in extent to their importance and dignity. As may be imagined, those early adventurers brought no fortunes with them, they were here to make them. A choice site selected, with cheap labor and material, wide-spreading adobe mansions were speedily erected with all the appurtenant structures, and far distant from encroaching neighbors, the lord of the manor was monarch of all he surveyed. From necessity and from choice it was a pastoral life. Numerous dependents flocked around him from the abandoned Indians and half-breeds, easily supported from the results of their own labor with the rapidly increasing flocks and herds and the limited cultivation of choice areas of rich bottom lands. There were a few years doubtless of struggle and trial, but these were safely negotiated, as immigration increased, and with the resulting large market, there came a boundless tide of prosperity for the ranchers. Whether under normal conditions the rain of wealth would have long continued is a matter of pure speculation. It came to a sudden and violent end with the drought of 1864-5, a catastrophe akin in its destructiveness to the march of an army, "somewhere in Europe" today. The vast herds of the county were almost exterminated and the ranchers reduced in a few months from great wealth to comparative poverty. As an instance, one of the most prominent among them, owned in the spring of 1863, over 200,000 head of grown cattle. He was offered $24 a head for them but refused to sell. At the end of 1864, he had but 800 cattle left, all the rest had perished from starvation. It was not an isolated case. The disaster was general. It had the unexpectedness of an earthquake. There was no record or tradition of such a dire happening in the county since its creation. But advised of the peril "preparedness" was the order of the day at least as to those who survived the storm. Many disappeared entirely as financial factors and lost their possessions. The more prominent ranchers realized that the pastoral era had passed and with the increasing values of land other avenues to fortune must be sought. Stock-raising must merge in dairying, herds must be improved and protected, and crops raised for their support. And with the fences, field and enclosures, dairies and barns that now followed the division of the great ranchos, it became the general custom with the provident farmers and dairymen to make due provision for the possible recurrence of a great "drouth." This was often in the shape of immense stacks of hay, not infrequently located on hilltops and enclosed with wire fencing. These stacks sometimes remained untouched for several years, curious objects in the landscape and grim reminders of past misfortune.

Under the changed conditions, many of the great ranchos were subdivided and passed to new owners, a new class, new to the country and its possibilities. They were open to conviction and prone to experiment, and satisfied on the whole that anything in the nature of vegetable production was possible in this virgin soil. The major industry following the stock era and its decline was dairying and the dairymen found no difficulty in adapting their methods to the new conditions and getting huge returns from the cultivation of barley, oats and rye for the needs of their cattle and to meet the growing demand of the rapidly increasing immigration.

Among other efforts to induce immigration and to acquaint the denizens of the effete East with the attractions of California, lecturers were sent far and wide at the expense of interested parties, lavishly supplied with literature on the subject and with photographs of the country. In these efforts San Luis Obispo was a leading attraction. Early in the '70s, an audience had gathered in a New England town to be entertained by one of these missionaries. A succession of plates was thrown upon the screen, in size and finish not dissimilar to the panoramic views shown in the moving picture shows today. To the surprise and amusement of certain people in the gathering, there presently appeared a "close-up" view of a harvesting scene, taken quite near San Luis Obispo in which they readily recognized relatives of theirs directing the operations of a great threshing machine. Far to the horizon stretched the sea of tall wheat, steadily the big gang of men labored at their several duties from the cutting of the grain to the sewing of the filled sacks and most characteristic of all, were the mountains of sacked wheat, piled high in orderly layers, there to remain for months in perfect safety from the elements. The incident is in point as illustrating the swift advance in agricultural methods in the county at that early date and the character of the new population.

Diversified farming rapidly followed. With improved roads and better transportation facilities, markets were more readily reached and the exports of grain and other products assumed large proportions. Flour mills were constructed in different parts of the county, but as the business developed capitalists became interested and costly mills with skilled operators and the latest methods and machinery supplanted the earlier ventures. After some years, in fact by natural evolution, one of the largest corporations on the Pacific Coast, having great flouring mills in its several states, in turn

71

absorbed the business in this county, and while incidentally supplying the local demand for flour and like breadstuffs, has since that time purchased the larger part of the grain raised in the county, the wheat it is claimed having peculiar excellences and making flour of special value.

As has been stated, the lands of the county differ widely in value. There are areas of broken country, difficult even of access, there are expanses of sand dunes, there are valleys of marvelous fertility. The problem before the new settler was to determine the most profitable use to be made of his land. If it was so valuable intrinsically that the return in any given industry could not be made to yield adequate revenue upon its capitalized worth, he naturally sought more profitable employment for it and on lesser acreage. All of which is obvious enough but is mentioned to emphasize the conditions confronting the immigrant from the far East where the lands might vary in character from fairly good alluvial to barren rock, or the man from the middle West with its boundless prairies, everywhere practically identical in its nature. But here, with a climate which barred only products purely tropical, it was a matter of soil and location. Adjoining tracts might differ radically. Only experiment would demonstrate what each was specially adapted for. That ascertained its value was settled. Sheep and cattle raising, dairying and grain raising were successively abandoned as the lands used for those industries proved too valuable for them. To illustrate, a few miles south of the county seat lies the valley of the Arroyo Grande, a stream running westward to the ocean from its sources in spurs of the Santa Lucia Mountains. During the summer months, it is by no means the "big river" that its name imports, but it drains a wide area and its powerful flood in past ages has brought down a vast amount of silt and has created a wide valley with the rich deposit. About this fertile expanse are rolling hills of all grades of agricultural value, some buried under sand dunes blown and drifted in from the ocean; some fit only to grow the dense chapparal which covers it but generally, however, of good character. But the valley land is incomparable. A good many years ago, eastern seed houses, as a bait to their customers, made a practice of offering premiums to them for the largest production from the seed sold them. They were finally obliged to bar out the Arroyo Grande farmers from the competition and were quite justified in doing so. They were confronted with an onion 26½ inches in circumferance and weighing 6 pounds and 14 ounces; with the record of 66,915 pounds of Wethersfield onions from one acre; with a seven-acre tract producing an average of 1,200 bushels of onions per acre, 100 of which weighed 408 pounds; with beans going 85 bushels; potatoes, 700 bushels; squash, 60 tons; beets, 70 tons; carrots, 100 tons; all to the acre, with potatoes weighing 10 pounds; radishes, 26½ pounds; carrots, 40 pounds; table beets, 50 pounds; mangel-wurtzel beets six feet long, 154 pounds; cabbages, 93 pounds; squash, 272 pounds each. A field of mangel-wurtzel beets resembled a mass of piles driven as the foundation for a sky-scraper building. However much these portentous growths may remind one of the abnormal and sinister productions imagined by Mr. H. G. Wells, that master of the amazing, in one of his works, yet conceding that they were phenomenal and unusual, they serve to indicate the singular fertility of the soil, which is the matter in question. These growths were due to no trick of the farmer, to no use of fertilizers. They were the prize exhibits at the old fairs or elsewhere duly sat upon by juries of horny-handed and envious competitors and so their recorded fame survives unchallenged. Besides exciting admiration and emulation, and securing prizes, some of these remarkable vegetables were instrumental in inducing immigration. They were exhibited in San Francisco and elsewhere and excited great interest. Mr. Horace Annesley Vachell, the celebrated English novelist and playwright, in his late work, "The Triumph of Tim," depicts graphically and amusingly the effect upon the hero of the book, of such a display. A wanderer in the Pacific metropolis seeking a new destination, he precipitately determines to seek the source of such prodigal gifts of Nature. Mr. Vachell, in this instance, is weaving memories of his own into the fabric of his fiction. Just such an experience changed his career and made him for many years a San Luis Obispoan, during which time he was a considerable factor in the growth of the county.

These lands of exceptional fertility (they are not all confined to the particular locality referred to) have historical interest as well. They were in one instance at least, the theater of exceptional sociological experiment. In the days of frenzied financial schemes in California, connected with the sale and subdivision of great tracts of land, days which it may regretfully be said have not yet ended, the accepted program was to take from the optimistic buyer, whatever small percentage of the purchase price he might be able to give and then abandon him to his own devices. Not infrequently, experiment demonstrated the hopelessness of the venture and his contract cancelled, his first payments forfeited, the unwary buyer moved on. Sometimes the individual was quite dissatisfied, considered himself defrauded and expressed his opinion in language that was forcible if not awful. Probably his unseemly violence was entirely justifiable. But there were transactions on much the same lines which disposed of the rich bottom lands with entirely different results. On them there are today, highly cultivated farms, the title to which is derived from a contract under the provisions of which the landowner not only exacted no part payment on the purchase price but even furnished the entire capital with which to clear the land and cultivate it until the net profits should have paid for the land and refunded all advances. The proposition was not without audacity in both parties to it. For the bottom lands in their native condition were densely overgrown with a jungle of willow, an impenetrable mass of vegetation. It was correctly assumed that it would cost $25 per acre to clear away this "monte." To this was to be added $75 per acre as the purchase price. The investment further involved the cost of the improvements, buildings, fences, stock, implements, seed, feed, farm and family support for a series of years. For a forty-acre tract it meant incurring an indebtedness of many thousands of dollars. Failure meant years of wasted effort for the purchaser. But aside from that possibly wasted effort the grantor in the transaction assumed all the financial risk and according to the iron rule which chiefly obtains in the affairs of men, he might have kept the last paring of profit for himself or in the absence of profit have gained by the gratuitous labor of his supposed purchaser. But in this instance there were no risks. The vegetable crops of a single year went far towards cancelling all indebtedness. Had the same prices prevailed then as in this current year of submarines and high cost of living, a single acre would have been sufficient for the purpose. These exceptional contracts were not numerous. They are only mentioned because they were unique and because the character of the soil made them possible and resulted satisfactorily to the purchaser. They ceased as the county became better known and immigrants of a different financial status multiplied. The experiments in "truck-farming" and other specially remunerative classes of production which followed the subdivision of the great ranchos proved the practicability of raising nearly everything which was not purely tropical, but by the process of selection, the general efforts in intensive farming were ultimately directed and confined to a limited number of products from which large uniform results might be depended upon. Boston and San Luis Obispo, divided by the width of the continent are strongly linked together by their mutual interest in beans, a limitless supply meeting an equally unlimited demand.

74

The seed farms of the county although not extensive are worthy of note, the wide acres of blossoming plants exhibiting masses of lovely colors. Of growing importance are the horticultural interests of the county, of which Mr. Guy E. Heaton, until recently county fruit inspector, speaking with the authority of practical experience for the past twenty-nine years, says:

Like most parts of California, San Luis Obispo County is singularly lacking in native fruits and nuts. These are represented by a few species of berries, mostly inedible, cherries and the black walnut. The cherries are of no value for food but some of the species are evergreens and make very desirable ornamentals, while the native black walnut is now considered the best stock for the cultivated walnuts.

This native poverty seems the more singular since no known territory is more readily responsive to horticultural effort or adapted to a wider range of products in this line.

There appears no evidence that the natives, before the advent of the Spaniards, practiced any sort of agriculture, but subsisted on Nature's products, so it is fair to presume that the padres introduced the first fruits, planting them contemporaneously with the missions.

That these fruits found a congenial situation is well attested by the fact that within the limits of the city of San Luis Obispo are yet standing many trees of different kinds still vigorous and fruitful, surviving the stress of changing ownership and lack of care, and which were planted in the mission gardens in the early days of Spanish occupation.

As homes were established beyond the missions, plantings were made at many of them, and in the absence of the different pests of tree and fruit now expected as a matter of course nearly every sort of fruit available was found adaptable, except citrus fruits, in those parts where the cold of winter is most severe.

With the American occupation tree planting was more rapidly increased and the coastal sections from the mountains down had larger or smaller plantings at nearly every ranch. Little care was required to produce enormous crops of fine fruit and this continued until the coming of the scale and other pests, and there seems to have been neither knowledge, resource nor inclination to control them. The farmers of the interior upon whose custom these plantings depended for a market had in the meantime made plantings of their own, and depended less and less upon others for a supply. These two causes meant the decline of the coast orchards. Of these old orchards that have survived most are in very poor condition, but where the owners are taking enough interest to care for them properly, they have shown a wonderful power of recuperation. However, the great profits realized from dairying in most of this part of the county, will doubtless hold it back from extensive fruit growing for some time, while in the interior it increases at a most satisfactory rate.

In the early '90s came a planting fever and tens of thousands of trees were planted in the Salinas Valley and adjacent territory. These were mostly prune and made good growth and fruitage, but the market for the fruit went to pieces, and after a few years of this the planters in despair abandoned or pulled up the trees and grain, and farming again held sway. Since the advanced price of prunes now ruling, some of these old orchards, after years of neglect, have been pruned and cared for and bring an annual revenue of several hundred dollars per acre.

San Luis Obispo County has several hundred thousand acres of the best of fruit lands. Practically all of this is adapted to pears, which are reputed the best grown anywhere, being grown without irrigation and standing up under cold storage far better than irrigated pears. Next to the pear the prune is most universally adapted and the high sugar content makes it of the best in the state. The peach too is almost universally grown and is of rare quality when grown not too near the coast. Apricots and walnuts are best on the coastal side. Arroyo Grande apricots are famous along with many other fruits grown there. There are perhaps 50,000 acres of the finest apple lands within the county. That apples unexcelled by any in the state or perhaps within any western state can be produced upon these lands, seems well proved by the fact that apples from the Laurel Glen Orchards have taken over sixty first prizes at three successive seasons of the California Apple Show. Laurel Glen is situated in the midst of the largest tract of these lands, which extend nearly the length of the county, lying on both sides of the Santa Lucia range but mostly on the interior side.

Although apricots and walnuts appear to find the coast soil and climate most congenial, good orchards of each are growing in the interior. Here during the past few years have been planted several thousand acres of almonds, and thousands more are proposed for this coming season. The thrift of the young orchards and the sure bearing and productiveness of the older ones show ideal conditions for this kind of horticulture, and there is a steadily increasing demand for lands adapted to it at increasing prices, which are still remarkably low when the profits shown are considered.

Impractical men have said that horticulture is a difficult art to practice in this part of the country, but with the right methods employed the reverse is true; trees are as easily grown here without irrigation as elsewhere with irrigation and with less expense. The list of fruits grown to perfection without irrigation is certainly remarkable. The following list shows only part of them: apples, peaches, pears, all sorts of plums and prunes, apricots, quinces, figs, all kinds of grapes, most sorts of berries including gooseberries, blackberries, loganberries, dewberries—all these grown over a very wide area within the county—almonds and walnuts within a smaller area, and citrus fruits within the thermal belts along the mountains and even in some of the valleys like the one in which San Luis Obispo lies.

Until a few months ago this county had no horticultural commission. Then Prof. Carl Nichols was appointed and immediately began a survey of the orchards. These were found remarkably free from the more serious pests, excepting scale of several kinds, on the coast and a few slight infestations in the interior, which latter were eradicated. It is to be expected that in view of the immense importance of its work that the commission will have financial allowance to enable it to work successfully.

The future of the fruit industry here depends upon the market. It is fully demonstrated that the commercial sorts and of the best quality can be as easily produced here as in the most highly favored localities elsewhere, excepting citrus fruits, raisins and perhaps a few others. For dried fruits and nuts the outlook is satisfactory; for the green fruits better facilities for transportation and marketing must come. This will no doubt be accomplished by the farm bureau, just organized in this county.

To one who has been through these many years of pioneering and experienced their incidental phases of success and disappointment, the outlook seems indeed cheering.

CHAPTER X

METALS AND MINERALS

Although San Luis Obispo County is preeminently agricultural in its pretensions and quite contentedly so, yet it is also extensively mineralized. Had the original proprietors known just what might have been obtained in the line of mineral wealth some Cortez or Pizarro might have led a gang of marauders here two centuries before occurred the peaceful pilgrimage of Padre Serra. The conquistadores were not looking for arable land and colonies in the modern acceptance of the word were valueless to them. They sought only the treasures of the mine, masses of precious metals, the sudden acquisition of vast wealth. Vaca crossed the continent from Florida to Texas; Coronado explored our great West from Texas to Kansas but these tremendous explorations were counted as worthless. Viscayno made his splendidly successful voyage of discovery along this coast but his report to his sovereign is a confession of failure. In vain he paints in glowing colors the manifold attractions of this vast new land and particularly of this section of it. His note is not triumphant, he scents disappointment in his royal master and finally he is fain to say that "the natives are well acquainted with gold and silver and claim that there are vast deposits thereof in the interior." Which did not sound convincing and probably was untrue. Nuggets of gold the Indians might have chanced upon in this county but free silver was not possible. Long years afterwards, so the myths run, the Spanish priests found and worked deposits of silver and there are tales still extant of "Lost Mines" of the padres but they were never found and silver is one of the few metals of which there is but scanty record. Gold too was a late discovery, although a score or more of years before Marshall's day, the metal had been found in considerable abundance in the southern counties of California and many thousands of dollars worth in lumps and dust were garnered by the trading vessels. This was placer gold, obtained from the streams in these central coast counties. The deposits in this county seem not to have been generally known until about 1878.

The auriferous region is on the eastern slope of the San Jose Mountains in the vicinity of La Panza. Long before the date mentioned gold had been found there but at that time for some reason, an "excitement" was created and goldhunters came in from all quarters. Hundreds came at the call of the "new strike" but they found as had the few who had preceded them that while gold could be found in the beds of the streams in that region and in paying quantities yet because of the scarcity of water, operations were unprofitable. Prospectors and geologists agree as to the existence of a vast deposit of goldbearing cement gravel which in the northern counties of the State, where the water supply is adequate would have great value. The gold is there but it is inaccessible. There have been favorable years of unusual rainfall and watchful claimowners have taken the utmost advantage of it, even hauling the pay gravel long distances to water. And in spite of such seemingly insurmountable difficulties, some degree of success has been attained. The records of the express companies show shipments of the gold amounting to over a hundred thousand dollars. But it is really a proposition for "hydraulicing." Nothing yet discovered but the onrush of a powerful stream of water will dissolve that mountainous mass of earth and rob it of its treasures. Gradually the miners abandoned their hopeless and ill-paid efforts but there are still a faithful few abiding there for whom those millions buried in the earth have an invincible attraction and who at least eke out an existence. And there are still others, landowners in the vicinity, to whom the mining is incidental but who carry it on systematically when conditions are favorable and obtain from it a quite regular revenue.

Assuredly the Spanish during their occupation of the country knew of no gold or silver in it, legends to the contrary notwithstanding. If they had discovered it, corroborative evidence would have existed as in Mexico. In working the mines, employment more profitable for their masters would have been found for the natives than in doing odd jobs about the Missions. The Commandantes Gefe Politico and other gentry of the secular arm would have been keenly interested. There would have been extensive workings and concealment would have been impossible. But there were other mineral deposits of which it is of record that the intelligent priests had noted but which unfortunately they could not develop. They knew of the existence of quicksilver and of copper but undoubtedly the mining and reduction of the ores was deemed impracticable or if not would perhaps at that time have been unprofitable. As a matter

79

of fact like conditions have obtained in more recent times and the fortunes of the mines have wavered with the rise and fall of the price of the metals in the market. The deposits of cinnabar in the county are of great extent and real importance. Fortunes have been expended in the last fifty years in exploiting them and in the erection of furnaces, etc., and at times with the rosiest prospects of rich returns. But quicksilver has always been an uncertain quantity, its supply and demand subject to the wildest vagaries and the fortunes which seemed so brilliant and so assured when the metal was quoted at $1.50 a pound vanished utterly as the price steadily dropped until it was far below the local cost of production. Mines and machinery were abandoned and work suspended for years but always the latent certainty that with recovered value, the metal would again pour from the furnaces. Which was but recently demonstrated when the world-war created the hoped-for demand and at once from all its mouths the cinnabar region streamed with the lustrous metal. The ore is found quite extensively along the eastern slope of the Santa Lucia Range in the northern part of the county. Serious and extensive work has been done in many locations chiefly by San Francisco capitalists.

The beginnings of actual development of the metal quite duplicated in its leading features, although on a smaller scale, the "strikes" that have marked the opening of new mining districts in other parts of the Pacific coast.. There was the wandering Mexican displaying samples of ore and curious as to its value; the alert American, quick to recognize the possibilities of happy fortune, the frenzied rush for possession and the staking and recording of hundreds of "claims." Presently on a few of the locations deposits were disclosed of large extent and we have a repetition of the tale of unscrupulous efforts to gain the ownership of them. In one instance and the story is quite authentic, the locators gave an option of purchase on their mine to certain individuals who at once departed for the metropolis to secure the support of capitalists to fulfil their contract of purchase and develop the property. But their errand became known, and when having succeeded in their efforts, the gentlemen returned to comply with the terms of their option, they found that regardless of their agreement, the locators had sold out to other parties.

Another of the mineral deposits of the county, which because of the great war has become valuable is chromium. This is found chiefly in the San Luis Range and its spurs, in the vicinity of the county seat, and is quite extensively distributed, sometimes occurring in large masses. As it usually lies near the surface and then requires but little skill or capital to mine it, the working of the various openings was chiefly for years in the hands of farmers or teamsters at times when their labor and teams could not be more profitably used. Pure chromium was of course highly valuable even when it was chiefly used as a pigment and its value increased as it became more widely used. But the reduction of the crude ore, the separation of the chromium from the iron and other metals with which it is found combined, was a difficult process, involving large investment of capital. The demand for the metal being limited, such reduction works were few in number and were able to fix their own price for the crude ore which of course was no larger than was necessary. It was so carefully figured that the return to the miner barely sufficed to encourage him to persist in the work. The chief cost to the reduction works, located in Philadelphia or that vicinity, was the freight, which from this county, although the ore was carried usually in ballast in sailing vessels around the "Horn," was greater than from Asia Minor. That part of the world was years ago about the only section where the ore was found in large quantities. At the present time there are deposits of far greater extent in other parts of the world. But then the price paid was predicated on the rate which had to be paid on the foreign ore. And that in turn had to include a small duty imposed by our tariff laws. Related to which last item was a business episode which was quite interesting to those concerned and the failure of which marked with some emphasis the cessation for many years of chrome mining in the county. As stated, a small percentage of the price paid for the ore at its destination in the Eastern reduction works accrued to the miners, the remainder was the cost of transportation. A very considerable part of the weight of the ore was due to the "country rock" in which the ore was imbedded and this subtracted the freight would be proportionately diminished to the benefit of the producer. So a profitable business venture presented itself. The opportunity was embraced and the necessary machinery obtained and installed. The ore was crushed and then finely ground and spread upon oscillating tables where it was washed clean and then dried and sacked for shipment. The process was simple, rapid and inexpensive and the financial results quite satisfactory. But unfortunately, after some months of prosperity, there was a sudden and entire collapse. The political complexion of the Government changed and chrome ore was put upon the free list. The principal promoter and manager of the San Luis Obispo enterprise was a sincere free trader and could only applaud this application of his principles but he had his personal and pecuniary regrets. The duty upon the foreign ore was small, it could not have perceptibly affected the ultimate cost of the mineral after reduction but it had been just sufficient to keep the mining industry in this county alive. Its repeal shut the doors of the local works and sent the plant to the scrap heap and caused the abandonment of the mines or quarries which had been in operation. Not until quite recently has it been profitable to reopen the mines. But the great war has changed the conditions. Chrome largely used in the manufacture of steel is in great demand and other uses no less important have been found for it. The submarine terror renders foreign importation precarious and costly and the native supply is being worked to the utmost. From the government records it appears that in the early days mentioned, 11,000 tons were shipped from the county in the year of greatest production. But the ore brought then only $8 per ton in San Francisco. At the present time the price obtained is from $20 to $30 per ton, depending on the content and demand is unlimited. "Five hundred carloads" is rumored as the order from one great steel works. With such alluring prospects, the old time record of production is being greatly surpassed.

Another mineral interest which has lain dormant for half a century since the first efforts made to develop it is a quite extensive deposit of iron and copper situated a few miles from the county seat and which experts report to be of great value. Its existence has been a matter of common knowledge from the earliest times but the absence of cheap fuel seems to have deterred capitalists from attempting its development. But the vast oil production has removed this obstacle and recently the effort has been renewed, much work has been done, furnaces are being erected and the abandoned tunnels of fifty years ago have ceased to merely remind the old settlers of the sanguine operators under whose orders they were made. The work ceased at his sudden death and his heirs not sharing his faith in the venture abandoned it.

But while as to most of the known metals and minerals, this county only shares their existence with other sections of California, there are others which are rarely found elsewhere as for instance alabaster and onyx. Still others are bitumen and bituminous rock. The bitumen is found in masses or as a heavy liquid welling up in "springs." At one time it was extensively used as a roofing material and the flat roofs of San Francisco's business blocks were quite generally made of it, covered with a thin coating of gravel. The bituminous rock is a curious combination of sand, lime and bitumen which softens by the application of steam and spread upon a proper foundation rapidly hardens and presents a surface of remarkable lasting qualities. Sidewalks and roadways made of it remain unimpaired for many years. Thousands of tons have been quarried and exported and used in the streets of San Francisco and even in Portland and the neighboring northern cities.

Petroleum at the present time figures so largely in the long list of the great productions of California that it seems hardly credible that it is only in comparatively recent times that it was known to exist here at all. And it was while its existence was still questionable and no notable development had been made in the state that a quaint character, who owned a small ranch a few miles south of the county seat, one day brought to town and exhibited a tin can filled with a dark, semi-fluid substance which he asserted was petroleum. He sought money to develop his discovery but in vain. He was considered a crank and finally abandoned his efforts. His incredulous friends unfortunately had gained their limited knowledge of coal oil from the fluid which filled their lamps. This substance submitted to them closely resembled the bitumen with which they were familiar. It was in fact a heavy oil, probably sixteen degrees gravity, with the asphalt base, characteristic of California petroleum. At the present time, thirty years later, the only oil produced in the county is being pumped from a system of wells, a short distance from that ancient discovery. But that is not because of any lack of persistent and costly effort to find it elsewhere. In the adjoining counties of Kern and Santa Barbara are located the richest oil fields in the state, and the proven territory extends to within a few miles of this county on either boundary. And when a decade or so ago, in this neighboring territory, the first experimental wells proved brilliantly successful, and further development had shown that there were vast areas of adjacent territory which was equally productive, it could scarcely be doubted that the adjoining lands in this county, not geologically dissimilar, would also prove oil-bearing. It was an interesting and exciting time. It was assumed that the southwest section of the county was the most favorable theater of action, but any precise location was a matter of speculation. The ablest experts and mineralogists could only look wise, talk learnedly of sinclines and anticlines and make long reports which were invariably favorable. Leases were obtained without difficulty, for it seemed to be considered that the more rough and broken, worthless and inaccessible the location, the better the chances for success, and the owners of such tracts seized with

83

avidity the unhoped-for chance to realize something, if only a promised royalty, from land which they had hardly reckoned as an asset. Stock companies were speedily formed and stock launched upon the "market," and it was only the very strong-minded who resisted the temptation to take a few blocks of stock. "Rigs" were erected and multiplied with marvelous rapidity and dotted the landscape and night and day drilling was diligently prosecuted. Favorable "prospects" were invariably met with, and when it became necessary to levy assessments to continue the work they were for a time quite cheerfully and generally met. But gradually after several years of persistent effort the excitement died out, new ventures

REFINERY AT OILPORT

met with but chilly reception and one after another the different companies ceased operations, went into liquidation and out of existence. Oil had been found in many of the wells, but only in small quantities. Oil sands had been penetrated in strata of remarkable thickness, but they were barren. The whole field had been explored and there was no uncertainty as to the results. Probably a quarter of a million of dollars was expended in the wholesale experiment, but the contributions had been so general and individually so limited that the loss occasioned no distress and but little complaint.

More extensive, even monumental, to all present appearances, was another disastrous venture connected with the oil production. On the bay shore, near the Village of Avila, a tract of many acres

84

in extent is covered with structures of brick and iron of varied and curious design. It is the plant of a great refining works which some years ago was erected by San Francisco capitalists, an investment, based, it is said, upon contracts connected with the oil production of Santa Barbara County and the contracts failing, the works were never put in operation. Kept intact, with jealous care, the costly buildings stand idle and unoccupied like a sleeping city, waiting some magic mandate of business to spring into life.

Quite another story is that of the utilization of the harbors of San Luis Bay as shipping points for the great oil fields of San Joaquin Valley. Great tankers, some of the largest constructed, are now being despatched in rapid succession from these ports, north, east and south, making it one of the greatest oil supply points in the world. "Topping" works are there, separating gasoline and distillate from the crude oil with a capacity of 15,000 barrels per day and from the fields of production, 150 miles away, through lines of six and eight inch pipe—600 miles of them—the crude oil is brought at the rate of 6,000 barrels daily. A number of pumping stations along the line as required force the heavy fluid to its destination and about twelve miles from the port is the "Tank Farm" where an accumulation of the oil is stored in reserve. The numerous great tanks and reservoirs in this repository have an aggregate capacity of some 7,000,000 barrels. Some of the receptacles are cylinders of steel, containing each 50,000 barrels or more set in orderly fashion, but at respectful distances apart. And some have earthen walls, and under their roofs are veritable lakes of oil, over 2,000,000 barrels. Distant as is the "Farm" from the port, it is within the range of possibility, because within the range of the huge guns carried by the modern battleship, that some hostile power might drop a few ponderous shells on these acres of combustibles. It is hardly imaginable, and yet there is today the note of war in the khaki-clad gentry, thickly posted around the grounds and pacing their rounds as keenly alert as if on picket duty "somewhere in France."

These pages are intended to sketch the activities of the people of the county rather than to catalogue its resources, otherwise some extended mention might be made of the many other mineral deposits believed to be important, but which are still undeveloped and are without the necessary human interest. Such, for instance, as the extensive saline lakes in the Salinas Valley, from which that valley and the river which takes its birth in the vicinity derive their name and which have been exploited only to meet the homely uses of the ranchers of the valley. Or the numerous mineral springs found in many parts of the county; of its lime and cement, of its granites and other building material. And besides space and time are lacking. We may at least add that from the neighboring hills has been quarried the granite which has been extensively used in our major city and that a scar of small dimensions, visible on the landward side of Morro rock, marks the place from which some hundreds of thousands of tons of granite have been quarried and lightered a few miles down the coast and cast into the ocean to form the breakwater constructed by the United States Government to protect the harbors in San Luis Obispo Bay.

CHAPTER XI

EDUCATIONAL

In this region, as in most parts of the Spanish or Mexican dominions, teaching the young idea how to shoot and the subsequent training of the mentality evoked, was, until the American occupation, quite generally regarded as essential or desirable for the scions of the upper classes only. The lower the rank in the scale of humanity, the more rudimentary the intelligence, the more obvious the need, the less, according to the theories of the ruling powers, should be expected the aid of the schoolmaster. It was the working hypothesis that the human race consisted of many very different kinds of animals, and each kind might reasonably be expected to remain in the mental station in which it was born. Much may be said and, in fact, has been said in favor of this philosophy. To argue against it is to preach discontent, so fatal to happiness. When the human animal is of a yellow or brown or black complexion, he has always been recognized at once by the white race as distinctively inferior and as a general thing quite incapable of escaping from his lowly condition. Until very recent times in accordance with this view, the care-free aborigine, whether native of Africa or India, America or the isles of the sea, in spite of centuries of contact with his lighter colored brother, has escaped the thralldom of the schoolroom. The natives of this section were equally fortunate. The kindly priests assumed, no doubt correctly, that the Indians they encountered had souls of average value, which would be eternally benefited, saved in fact, by the knowledge and acceptance of the true faith. To accomplish this sacred purpose, their dim and doubtful mentality had to be reached, but no unnecessary demands were made upon it. It was less an appeal to reason than to sensibility. It was perhaps a clarifying of the vague and formless religion already latent in their minds. It was certainly the instilling of a profound faith in the divine mission of the priest as the special messenger of the deity, irreverence for whom would be impiety and sacrilege, and the creation of a mystic devotion through signs and symbols, forms and ceremonies. But the training was by no means superficial. It may be that the native races of California, of Mexico and Peru, docile, peaceable and credulous, were peculiarly amenable to priestly influences. Certainly there were some of the tribes in Arizona and Eastern California who were not so easily handled and who were considered by the Spaniards as sons of Belial and the offspring of Shytan, fit only for extermination. But with our coast Indians as with the great multitude of the natives of the Spanish new world, the dominion of the priests was established with miraculous ease, and so solidly that the chances and changes of the centuries have not availed to shake it. It became universal throughout the vast region of the Spanish occupation and has remained so. It is not too much to say that the priests were Spain's real "conquistadores" in America. For Spain in the sixteenth century was not equal, from a military standpoint to so great an achievement. Only at that period in fact had she become a nation. In territory or population she was hardly larger than is California today. Surrounded by war-like neighbors, her armies and her limited resources were required for her own salvation and could hardly be ventured in doubtful schemes of conquest in lands so distant. The small bands of soldiery which formed the early expeditions, even with the advantage of armor and firearms, would have been uselessly sacrificed in contending with masses of hostile natives, if they had relied solely upon their own prowess. But the priests were the pioneers and in their foosteps the invaders could follow with safety.

Although there was a great lapse of time between the earliest expeditions of the Spaniards and the venture of Father Serra through this region, the conditions were practically the same. There was again a civil and military force largely in evidence, but so far as history discloses, of no practical value but more often an irritating nuisance. There were codes of laws automatically creating civic conditions but it does not appear that they were or could be usefully applied and they were not. And there were hordes of natives to be dealt with in some wise. The ambitions of the regal gentlemen at Madrid decreed the adventure in the interest of territorial expansion but the practical solution of the problems involved fell as before to the lot of the priest. It was required to make a fixed and productive population out of the natives, the only available material. The simple but eminently successful program of the priest was to educate the aborigine. The course of study was not extensive. It had two branches. The one, which might be considered the intellectual was devoted to the implanting of

88

religious principles and practices and the other might be called, in modern parlance, the "vocational." As before intimated the pupil had already some rudimentary notions in both branches. He was not devoid of religion although his conceptions might be vague, erroneous and defective and a certain skill in handicrafts and culture of the soil had been necessary to his existence. This system of education gave quite satisfactory results; true religion became universal and the padre's polytechnic school graduated the native population en masse, as well-skilled in all the arts and crafts known to their teachers. But the three "Rs" formed no part of the curriculum. That such knowledge was too dangerous for the natives to possess was the view stubbornly maintained by the authorities, church and civil. Years later, Echeandea, the first of the Mexican governors and somewhat of a progressive politically, finding that only a small proportion of the population could read, endeavored to institute universal and compulsory education to that extent but without success. He seems to have been regarded as a public enemy on that account and his erroneous educational notions counted largely in creating an unpopularity that finally ousted him from his exalted position and from the country.

The children of the white people fared differently. Schools of high degree there were none but attached to the staffs of the civil and military functionaries were clerks and secretaries who could be made useful as tutors in the families of their patrons and quite commonly the scions of the wealthier officials were sent to seats of learning in South America, Mexico or old Spain. Considering such difficulties besetting the pathway to knowledge, the degree of culture and refinement attained and maintained through succeeding generations was remarkable. There are yet living those who remember the pure-blooded descendants of the Spaniards, the native Californians of the better class who figured largely in the early days of the American occupation. The old pioneers can testify to the keen intelligence, the considerable attainments and the courtly bearing which was the common possession of those colonial grandees. It redounds to the credit of their progenitors, that posted as they were upon the frontiers of the new world, abandoned to their own resources, they should have handed on the torch of learning and civilization unquenched and undiminished in lustre for so many generations. There are cherished manuscripts in state archives and private libraries that have survived the ravages of time and which give interesting evidence of the intellectual status of those old Spanish adventurers. Something too might be said of their skilled penmanship which seemed to be quite a common accomplishment. Poor chirography does not necessarily indicate lack of mental power, e. g. Horace Greeley or Shakespeare or Bonaparte and an elegant penman may be only a good writing master but the nervous rapid script of the intelligent, educated writer is unmistakable, although appearing merely in an official document.

In the wake of the Yankees came of course the "little red schoolhouse" or at least what the phrase connotes, the open door to the halls of learning. In this county it was red by tradition only, the color did not suit the climate. In the earliest days there was not always a house. There is a delightful memory of one academy a least whose roof was only a wide-spreading oak, under whose shade were grouped teacher and pupils on primitive benches and there, in the clear air, the brilliant sunshine and the gentle breezes, during the long rainless months, in such ideal conditions, in peace and pleasantness, the joyous band of children gathered at the sound of the school-going bell. But schoolhouses were rapidly constructed. Race suicide had not been invented in those early days, children swarmed and were a first consideration. Usually the edifices erected were inexpensive as the property-owners in the district had to meet the cost by direct taxation or bond issue and were not inclined to extravagance in architecture. There was an occasional exception. One is remembered that occasioned some malicious hilarity. The schoolhouse erected was really an imposing structure for the time and place, far and away the most pretentious in the district. It seemed a splendid monument to the self-sacrifice of the inhabitants and to their high appreciation of the value of education. For nearly all of them apparently were housed in cheap shacks on scattered quarter sections around the margin of the district and their largest available and visible asset seemed to be children and dogs. Fully explained, however, their self-sacrificing spirit was less obvious. For most of the valuable area of the district was the property of absentee owners, locally represented by cattle and vaqueros chiefly and of the cost of the desired building only a negligible fraction was saddled upon the resident settlers. The condition was not an isolated one. The larger area of the most available lands in the county was covered by the wholesale grants, which to a great extent ultimately fell into the hands of absentee owners or were held intact to the exclusion of small settlers and it was but just and a reasonable contribution to the upbuilding of the community that those owners should pay their larger proportion of public requirements of all kinds, schoolhouses in particular. And

90

it is but fair to say that there was but rarely any lack of public spirit exhibited by the great landowners but on the contrary they made commendable efforts in aid of the newer civilization. The post of pioneer teacher was not without its difficulties of all kinds in those days. The native population was very largely in the majority and the language of the country was Spanish. The county was still in many respects a Mexican province. Spanish was spoken exclusively in the courts and public offices and was used for all records and conveyances. English had to be the "major study" in the schools. Teachers however seemed to have been found without difficulty. And in the course of time there were recruits to the educational force that were noteworthy. Among them was Edwin Markham, who as he has told us, was first inspired to write his wonderful "Man with the Hoe," and made the first draft of it, when he was teaching a little public school in this county, although years were to pass before the perfected effort was to be given to the world. And of lesser lights there were many young men who strayed into this field and who here or elsewhere achieved more or less distinction. Among them was "Charley" Shinn, whose writings are widely known. Levi Rackliffe, who became state treasurer; F. E. Darke, J. M. Felts and W. M. Armstrong, successively superintendent of the schools of the county. There were financial difficulties as well. For some years the entire support of the schools was a direct charge upon the taxpayers and it was not until the '60s that the magnificent endowment of the state came to their aid. Thereafter the network of the school districts was rapidly extended to cover the entire county and in due course of time, graded and high schools were added and the system put upon a par at least with the most advanced sections of the state. Private schools were started from time to time but found little support except of course the Catholic Parish School under the management of the Sisters of the Order of the Immaculate Heart of Mary, always amply supported in their labor of love and religious duty.

Thus far has been recounted the gradual evolution of educational effort which being in the main, common to a greater or less degree, to all sections of the republic, is of interest to the casual reader only insofar as the conditions of changing populations and forms of government, have made it so. Of more general interest is the story of the establishment by the Legislature of the State of California Polytechnic School, a novel experiment in public school education and which while failing to some degree to meet the san-

91

guine expectations of its projectors, is still a satisfactory demonstration of the correctness of their theories.

It was in the session of the Legislature of 1900-1 that the bill was at last passed for the establishment of the school. At the session of 1896-7, an effort had been made by Senator S. C. Smith, whose district embraced this and the adjoining County of Kern, to have located in this county a normal school, which it had been determined by those in authority was to be created in addition to those already in existence. Citizens of the county on the alert and eager to seize any opportunity for its upbuilding, had prompted his action and Mr. Smith had very willingly acted upon their suggestion. He was glad to do so. He regarded himself as under special obligations to this part of his bailiwick as in truth he owed to it the majority which secured his election when his home county had failed him. The desire of his constituents was quite intelligible and creditable. As a decorative feature the school buildings with their customary palatial architecture would be a source of great pride and incidentally there would be financial benefit as well. Geographically and climatically, no other section could make superior claim. But however ideal the conditions and however desirous Mr. Smith might be to oblige our guileless citizens, he was quite well aware that the proposition was a hopeless one. For the normal school was a juicy prize upon the political plum tree and had been allotted to its destined beneficiary before even its intended creation had been made public. Nothing remained to be done about it except the mere formal legislation. Those were the palmiest days of the reign of King Mazuma. California had always had its full quota of political rascals but their predatory exploits had lacked that organization and discipline so essential to real and complete success in all human endeavor. There were large interests quite willing to share generously the loot they might gather through dark and devious ways in the larger cities or by legislative enactment but it was often annoying to have to meet the cumulative demands of isolated bands of freebooters. It created unreasonable expense and besides interfered with the circumspection and secrecy which were at all times most desirable. We can imagine that a friendly bond of union was equally satisfactory to the pot-hunting crowd whose livelihood was thus rendered less precarious in the comfortable assurance of due recognition of their abilities and liberal reward for their industry. It was an era of great content. Political convictions were practically ignored. One could be as serviceable under one banner as another. While the field of endeavor in the larger cities offered great opportunities for the gang, no pent up Utica confined their powers. The state, with its splendid revenues, its innumerable offices, commissions and institutions, more especially the halls of legislation, was far more fruitful in opportunity. The beneficial results of skilful combination were speedily apparent and the raw and crude efforts at bribery and corruption were superseded by more sophisticated methods. Affairs of moment for future legislation were settled at the primaries where judicious selection of candidates could be made for the support of the enthusiastic electorate. It was not difficult. Ambitious and unscrupulous aspirants for office were numerous and not unwillingly accepted assistance that enslaved them and these, with the talented rogues, the leaders in the ring, whose role was political preferment, made up an adequate working force in either house that might be depended upon to assure or defeat any required legislation. Senator Smith was a man of much political sagacity and while his conclusions might be based upon conjecture only, they sufficed him and convinced of the futility of contesting the accomplished fact of the disposition of the proposed normal school, he abandoned the effort and introduced the bill for the creation of the polytechnical school. His action was due to no sudden impulse. As explained by him, it was an endeavor to realize a vision to which he had given much study. He was distinctly one of the "plain people" and in his career as teacher, lawyer, journalist and politician, his natural predilections allied him closely with the struggling masses. He quite believed that all men were created equal mentally and that the wide variances existing in ability, efficiency and success resulted largely from lack of early mental training. Applying his theory to local conditions he noted that the vast majority of the boys of the state abandoned prematurely the systematic training of the schools and with the greater part of these the result was arrested mentality, the constant swelling of the ranks of the mere hewers of wood and drawers of water. His remedy was the free public trade school where the vast number inclined to mechanical pursuits would be led to accept the further training that was essential even to the material success which was their prime demand. In the polytechnic school for this county he planned no ornate buildings or park-like grounds. Only an array of workshops, plain, substantial structures conveniently grouped and amply supplied with all the tools and implements, machinery, apparatus and appliances of the various mechanical pursuits and

93

conducted by the ablest possible instructors. General instruction should have been secured in the existing public schools.

With a clear field, Mr. Smith might reasonably have expected the adoption of his plan. It had great merit. Largely by schools of practically the same character, Germany, before embarking upon its insane war, had reached a world-wide supremacy in industrial efficiency. He himself had great influence with his brother senators. He had the loyal and enthusiastic co-operation of the assemblymen from this district, both men of force and ability. But he had no illusions. He knew that he was not numbered with the elect and the way of the grafter was past finding out. No shadow rested on the disposition of the normal school bill yet its success was known in advance. No opposition was manifested to the polytechnic bill and still its fate was uncertain. Such bills carrying appropriation were always received hospitably. They provided for "logrolling." To gain support for them their proponents might be induced to reciprocate by the support of measures which they might otherwise have looked at askance. Even if there was no chance in them of gainful pursuit and their defeat was decreed, still there might be incidental pickings, warranting kindly treatment. There might be visiting delegations of amateur lobbyists, provided with limited sacks perhaps but who might furnish a select few with refreshments of various kinds. Then there might be junketing trips, affording legislative delegations agreeable excursion enlivened with banquets and much kowtowing and flattering articles in the local newspapers, all of which while having no earthly effect on the desired legislation, was a pleasing perquisite for the legislators.

The polytechnic bill followed this accepted program. With no marked opposition it passed the Senate and Assembly in the session of 1897 and was promptly vetoed by Governor Budd. Re-introduced in the session of 1899, it again wended its way through the Legislature with the same ominous placidity, reached Governor Markham and received his veto. Again in the session of 1901, the bill was presented and carried through with gratifying enthusiasm to Governor Gage—but he failed to veto it. Just why was never exactly understood. He had definitely announced his intention to do so. Mr. W. F. Herrin, currently understood to control the political management of the "interests" and to whose advice the governor would naturally pay great deference, had emphatically declared his hostility to the bill. But there was a sudden change of front and the bill was signed. Friends of the measure attributed the change to the kindly efforts of Mr. W. H. Mills who stood high in the Southern Pacific Railway councils and who had been successfully appealed to for assistance.

In the course of his long struggle for the adoption of his bill, Mr. Smith had been compelled to accept interpolations which would enlarge the scope of its activities so as to include agriculture and the training of girls in domestic work. He had urged strenuously that such additions would be destructive of the proposed school whose only reason for existence was free instruction in mechanical pursuits. To attempt agricultural work would only be to create a picayune rival to the great agricultural college of the State University, a hopeless and ill-advised effort and the interests of the young women were already adequately provided for in the existing grammar schools. But his protests were unavailing and he could only trust optimistically to the intelligent action of the directors to be appointed and whom he might hope to assist in selecting. But that hope was deceived. The directors appointed by the governor included a prominent member of the faculty of the State University, a wealthy gentleman of Santa Cruz, who was entitled to consideration for political services and a distinguished attorney of San Luis Obispo, a personal friend of Mr. Herrin, neither of whom were at all in sympathy with Mr. Smith's plan but proceeded on what they doubtless regarded as more practical and less Utopian lines. Their first effort was to secure a suitable location. To forestall any possible suggestion of graft in this direction, friends of Mr. Smith, at his suggestion had already secured offers of sites and among them one from Mr. J. D. Grant, widely known as a wealthy and public-spirited gentleman to whom the idea of the school strongly appealed. He offered to donate twenty acres of land and to sell any additional land adjoining which might be required for $100 per acre. The land offered was immediately beyond the south boundary of the town. It fronted on an excellent road, the continuation of the city street and now part of the "Camino Real." It was level; the soil rich and deep, abundantly watered and easily drained. Later, the county appraisers valued land in the vicinity of the same character at $350 per acre. There were a number of other locations proposed and the directors of the school finally selected a tract on the northern edge of the city. It was hilly, scantily supplied with water, the soil poor and thin. To the objection that it was not well adapted to agriculture the directors countered with the reply that that was a point in its favor. Anybody could succeed with good land. The teachers of agriculture would have the opportunity of demonstrating how to succeed with inferior soil. The real and decisive consideration for the directors appeared to be that the tract skirted the Southern Pacific Railway and the school would afford an object of interest to passing travelers. The location settled, the next step was the selection of a manager or superintendent, presumably a man of wide experience in polytechnic work and whose high standing and reputation would aid in successfully launching the new venture. The directors appointed a young collegian of pleasing manners and address who was an instructor in the Dairy School of the State University. Buildings were then erected upon the plans of a rural architect,

CALIFORNIA POLYTECHNIC SCHOOL, SAN LUIS OBISPO

picturesque in appearance but cheap and temporary in character and providing only class and recitation rooms and household accommodations for the faculty and others. Finally the curriculum was prepared. It was practically confined to agriculture and "domestic science." The trade school feature was chiefly "honored in the breach."

Mr. Smith viewed the melancholy fate of his bantling with amused disgust but he had been powerless to help it. It reminded him of the unhappy condition of the veteran of the Civil war, who had lost both legs and both arms and had suffered other frightful injuries. He was encountered shortly after the close of the great conflict by a Southern officer, who greeted him with the remark which was not intended to be as ferocious as it sounds: "Well, you're the first damn Yankee that I have met that was just trimmed up to suit me."

But although the initiatory measures taken seemed to augur badly for the success of the new institution as a trade school and would appear to make of it rather a preparatory school for the State University to which its graduates were early accredited, yet in the course of time the industrial features emerged and to a considerable extent have been taken advantage of. The school has prospered and has a hopeful future before it.

A novel departure in educational work in California, which has met with the enthusiastic approval of the school directors of San Luis Obispo County is what is known as the Junior College, a proposition which by statutory provision permits the extension of the courses in the high schools of the state to cover the freshman and sophomore years in the state universities, enabling the student to complete his college education with only two years' attendance at the university, a plan which has obviously many advantages.

Until a comparatively recent period, the intellectual training received in college was quite generally deemed essential only to the few who intended to follow one of the three learned professions. For others it was considered only ornamental if not detrimental. But times have changed and even in the most mechanical pursuits, and the mere struggle for material success, the lack of thorough education, best obtained in our higher institutions of learning, is felt to be a serious handicap. The result is seen in the vastly increased number of students in the universities. But the further result, it is claimed, is that in such huge institutions the student cannot receive the same individual attention and direction as in the smaller colleges of former days. The instructors in the Junior colleges being at present quite equal in pedagogical value to those employed in the lower classes of the universities and the course of study identical, the student has the advantage claimed of closer supervision and assistance, of remaining within home influences within the two years, usually a critical period in his life and with much less expense, often a deciding consideration.

With reference to the present status of the public schools of the county, Mr. A. H. Mabley, principal of the San Luis Obispo city schools, says:

A test of the completeness of the educational facilities of a community lies in their capacity to train every kind of mind. In so far as the practical mind, the meditative mind, the reasoning mind, the imaginative mind, the quick mind and the slow mind find particular means of development in a school system, in just so far is the system a complete one. Beginning with the primary department San Luis Obispo County schools offer educational opportunities through the usual grammar and high schools and ending with the Junior College.

The number of schools in the county is about 100, employing 175 teachers. The schools are scattered conveniently throughout the county, the state wisely providing support for districts that would otherwise be without the service of teachers. Each of these schools enjoys the instruction of from one to three teachers if in a rural district and as many as thirty-four in the county seat. The high

HIGH SCHOOL, SAN LUIS OBISPO

standard for teachers demanded by California laws guarantees that the teaching in the rural districts shall be comparable to that in the cities. Such districts are also favored by a law enacted through the efforts of Senator Rigdon, legislative representative from San Luis Obispo, providing for so-called post-graduate studies in rural schools, thus allowing children living in remote districts to secure at least the rudiments of a high school education.

There are four high schools in the county, enrolling about 400 students. The schools are located in Arroyo Grande, Templeton, Paso Robles and San Luis Obispo.

The courses given in these schools are similar to those to be found in the modern high schools throughout the country, consisting of English, mathematics, history, science and ancient and modern languages. In the larger ones such subjects as art, music, drawing, manual training and domestic science are taught as well as commercial courses including shorthand, typewriting, and bookkeeping. Any boy or girl can find material for his or her bent. The California Polytechnic School furnishes training in agriculture, mechanics and household arts. The San Luis High School provides complete courses in academic subjects and has recently added a Junior College department which enables high school graduates from any place in the county to secure the first two years of college work. This work is carefully inspected by the State University.

The tax-payers of the county provide a reasonable amount of money for their schools. The total amount spent on the schools for the fiscal year 1915-16 including state aid was $217,000. Of this $180,000 was spent on elementary, the balance on high schools. The per capita cost of educating elementary school pupils was $35.72, and high school pupils $124.00.

The instruction in the San Luis Obispo County schools is organized on the assumption that first of all the fundamentals of education should be taught. The "three Rs" must be the core of every successful elementary course of study for these are the subjects needed by every boy and every girl whatever his or her future may be. They are the backbone of education. But education need not stop here. Unless it is something more than a means of earning one's bread and butter, it has fulfilled only half of its function. A child must do many things besides earning a living. He must learn to express himself in correct language; he must come to know some little at least of the best literature that he may see visions beyond the daily humdrum tasks of life and receive some uplift from the world's great creative minds. He must acquire an intelligent comprehension of the earth and of the life upon it, of the character and location of its cities and countries; he must be made acquainted with the forces of life manifested in plant and flower and with that higher form of life exemplified in his own body. He should be taught some of the graces of life, and above all the noble principles of justice and morality. In brief, every well-directed course of study provides first a sound foundation for earning a livelihood, and second, a means of ennobling that living in terms of things worth while.

To fulfill these purposes the course of study in the elementary schools of the county includes, in addition to the fundamental subjects of reading, writing and arithmetic, the study of geography,

99

physiology, hygiene, grammar, literature, music, drawing, art, morals and manners. In the high and polytechnic schools of the county the boy and the girl find opportunity for development in every healthy direction. Through regular studies of the course the student may prepare for certain professions immediately or he may prepare for college. In addition opportunities are offered for activity in literary and musical work and in athletics. In a word the high school aims to develop its young people by the proper exercise of all their faculties, into upright, capable and efficient members of society.

The Junior College movement is ten years old. In 1907 the California Legislature passed an act authorizing boards of education to add two years to the regular four year high school course. The first school to take advantage of the law was the Fresno High School which established such a continuation school in 1910. Since that time the idea has been popularized until there are at the present time twenty-four such schools in the state. Among these is the San Luis Obispo Junior College, organized in connection with the high school last August.

The purpose of the Junior College system is to provide an accessible and economical means of securing the first half of a college education and also to satisfy community needs in providing advanced education in certain lines. In almost every community there are a number of high school graduates who desire to continue their education but who find it impossible through force of circumstances to travel so far and live so long away from home in order to secure it. If they are to secure it at all the college must be brought to them. This can sometimes be done with comparatively little expense, not by organizing a new institution but by extending the high school course already provided with the foundation and, if the choice of teachers has been fortunate, with instructors for such work.

The local Junior College was made possible by the offer of the teachers of the high school to serve as instructors in the college without extra compensation and by the keen interest of the board of education. The plan adopted was unpretentious, aiming to start with such academic courses as could be satisfactorily given with the equipment at hand. Courses have been given the past year in English literature and exposition, college algebra, modern European history, principles of economics, advanced Spanish and advanced Latin. These courses have been made equivalent to the corresponding courses in the regular colleges, being taught by instructors that have done post-graduate work in the leading uni-

100

versities of the country. Next year, in addition to courses in most of the above subjects, courses will be offered in art, political science, Greek and science.

The local Junior College is open to high school graduates on the same conditions as are required for entrance to the State University at Berkeley. Applicants who have within one or two of the required number of recommended grades are considered on their individual merits. There is no tuition, nor any charge except laboratory fees, to a resident of the county. The Junior College welcomes students from the county at large.

It is intended by the board of education and the school authorities that the Junior College shall become a feature of the city school system that will be of the greatest possible usefulness in extending higher education among the youth of the city.

The Junior colleges of the state are closely inspected by instructors and professors from the University who report their condition, in view of the amount of credit to be allowed their courses as compared with similar courses at the University. The local Junior College is organized on lines the aim of which is to fulfill the University requirements for advanced credit and assurance has been given that students that have taken the five full-year courses will be given full credit for the same at the University. Provided the standard is maintained, students completing the sixty-four credits in the same group of subjects as that required at the University will be able to enter the Junior year at Berkeley after two years at the local Junior College.

CHAPTER XII

RELIGIOUS

All early California history is inseparably linked with religious life and ideals. As on the Atlantic Coast the first settlements of our modern American civilization were due to religious motives, so on the Pacific Coast the foundations of civilization were laid on religious lines. There was this important difference, however, on the eastern coast the Pilgrim Fathers sought freedom from persecution on account of their religious ideals, while the Mission Fathers of the Pacific Coast braved privations and even death, in order to establish their faith by making converts of the natives. For that reason, the religious history of any community, particularly one where is located one of the old missions, is largely a history of the California missions.

While all modern California history begins with the period of the advent of the Mission Fathers, earlier explorers had visited this western coast and left behind them record of such visits. Juan Cabrillo was the first of these visitors. He explored the coasts of California in 1542-43, making several landings on the coast off what is now Santa Barbara and the islands adjacent thereto. Cabrillo dying during this voyage, it was completed by his successor, Farralo. This expedition examined the coast-line as far north as Cape Mendocino and made a number of visits to the natives that lived along the shores.

Sir Francis Drake made his famous visit to the California coasts in 1549, where "in a convenient and fit harbour" repairs were made to his ships and considerable intercourse was had with the surrounding native population. It was during this visit that there was conducted the first religious service of any sort ever held on the California coast. It was at a point near what is now known as Drake's Bay, north of San Francisco, that the Rev. Francis Fletcher, chaplain to Sir Francis, gathered the sailors of the several ships of the fleet, and attended by Drake in person, held a service on shore on the "first Sunday after Trinity, June 21st, 1549." Many natives assembled to witness this strange sight, which is commemorated by the "Prayer Book Cross," erected by Geo. W. Childs, late of Philadelphia, in Golden Gate Park, San Francisco.

A little over sixty years later, in 1602-03, Sebastian Vizcaino, a Spanish explorer, conducted a visit along the coast from which more knowledge of those early times is gained than from any of his predecessors. Vizcaino made visits to what later became known as San Diego and Monterey bays, and in January, 1603, visited the old Port of San Francisco, now known as Point Reyes. He made extended visits on shore and gathered much data and information regarding the natives. This ended all attempts of this character until more than a century and half had passed.

In 1767 the Jesuits were expelled from the missions on the Peninsular of Lower California and their supervision of this work was turned over to the Franciscan monks. At about this time the Spanish Government determined to carry out a long-projected plan for providing ports of supply for ships returning from the Orient, and also to occupy the land along the coast, against occupancy by Russians, or others. In the furtherance of this plan, it was decided to make use of the old ports of San Diego and Monterey, about which very little was known at the time, by sending troops and secular forces to take possession of them. The Franciscans, ever zealous in missionary efforts, took advantage of the opportunity and united forces with the secular arms of Government, in order to establish a chain of missions in Alta California similar to those on the lower peninsular.

The man chosen to head the missionary forces was Father Junipero Serra, one of the most interesting and saintly characters in American history. He was frail and slender in build, and much worn by constant labor in mind and body and in the practice of religious austerities. He had a brilliant career before him in his native land, but turning his back upon this, like the famous founder of the order to which he belonged, he sought honors not for himself but for his Master, in spreading abroad the knowledge of that Master. He determined to convert the natives of this far-off western coast to the Christian religion.

Four expeditions were planned whereby to effect the proposed settlement of the new land, by these combined secular and religious forces. These were organized in Mexico in 1769, to start for Upper California, two by land and two by sea. After innumerable trials and difficulties the two expeditions by sea succeeded in making San Diego Harbor. Among those accompanying the last land expedition were Governor Portola and Father Serra. The first ship arrived on

April 11, 1769, the last of the expeditions, one by land, arriving on July 16th.

The missionary features of these expeditions and the resultant missions, have often been criticized. Probably no one, not even the famous head himself, would claim them to have been perfect in every particular. Their members were human, and it is ever the lot of human beings to show some form of imperfection. Their motive, however, was above criticism. They were organized to convert the natives and to save human souls. It was a motive as pure as it was commendable. If the missions, some of them, later on became wealthy, that was due largely to the natural increase of the virgin soil. Similar wealth fell to the lot of the secular servants and citizens of the land. The missionaries all of them, left home and friends and opportunities for advancement in more congenial surroundings, in order to make their home in a far-away land and to live as aliens among strangers. Many of them lost their life, and in earlier days, all of them suffered many privations and much want.

But the work of these missionaries prospered abundantly. Eventually, twenty-one stations were established. The first of these was at San Diego, and was established July 16, 1769, the last one was at Sonoma, and was established April 25, 1820. They were all built on a general plan. Usually, the buildings were so arranged as to form the three sides of a square. The church occupied the middle section, and upon this building was expended the greater amount of effort at beauty in effect. The interior walls were as artistically adorned as circumstances would permit, and in many instances this interior decoration was so well developed as to have created a distinct ecclesiastical art of its own. The materials used in construction were according to what was most easily obtainable in the vicinity of the mission. Sometimes stone, occasionally wood, was used. More frequently however, the material was "adobe" or a sun-dried brick of good-sized dimensions fashioned out of the native soil. Many of the buildings display great skill in their erection, and much ingenuity in methods of construction. The old mission at San Luis Obispo, still extant, contains ceiling beams at least 10 inches square, and must have been made of timbers cut some thirty miles up the coast. How these heavy timbers were transported that great distance, or placed in the position they now occupy, no one living knows.

At a convenient distance from the church was the house occupied by the priest, and back of this usually, was placed the workshop and storehouses. Quarters for the Indians were located at some distance from the church, and frequently were very similar in construction to

104

those occupied by them in their native habitat. These quarters were called the "rancheria." Not far from the Indian quarters, was the "castillo" or building occupied by the soldiers, which usually consisted of a force of three or four Mexican soldiers. Their quarters were made as strong as possible in order to withstand attack from the Indians. In the earlier days there were frequently such attacks made by the still uncivilized natives. In connection with some of the missions were "presidios," or military quarters, maintained by the Spanish Government to preserve peace among the natives, as well as to repel any attack that might be made by foreign enemies.

Two of these missions are located in San Luis Obispo County. Several others in parts adjacent thereto. One of the missions in this county is that at San Luis Obispo, after which the city of that name is called. This was the fifth mission established and dates from September 1, 1772. The other mission is located at San Miguel and was the sixteenth mission established and bears the date of July 25, 1797.

There was also a mission station, at which occasional services were held, at Santa Margurita, about ten miles from San Luis Obispo.

A translation from the record from "Father Palou's Life of Padre Junipero Serra," made for the Tribune of San Luis Obispo, gives the following account of the founding of this mission:

"The founding of the mission was on the first day of September, 1772. Our venerable father said Mass under a bush arbor and setting out on the following day, i. e., the 2nd. of September, proceeded on his way to San Diego. He left at the mission two California Indians to assist, and the Senor Commandante, one Corporal, and four soldiers for protection. Because of his limited supply, he left for the padre, the five soldiers and the above-mentioned Indians, only two arrobas of flour and three almudes of wheat. And to purchase seeds of the Indians he left a box of brown sugar. Leaving the padre well contented with such a limited supply, placing his confidence in God, he set off on his journey"

The account of the service is as follows:

"On the 1st of September, 1772, Father Serra, assisted by Father Jose Caballar, blessed and put in place the holy cross. They then suspended a bell to the branch of a sycamore on the edge of the creek, and after ringing it some time to attract the attention of the Indians, one of the priests advancing, cried out: 'Ea! gentiles! venid! venid! a la Santa Iglesa! venid! venid! a recibir la fe de Jesu Cristo!' which translated means, 'O! gentiles! come ye! come ye! to the holy church! Come, come, and receive the faith of Jesus Christ!' The Indians understanding not a word that was said, expressed by their looks and gestures, however, the utmost astonishment. Mass was then sung amid a vast concourse of Indians. Thus was founded the mission of San Luis Obispo de Toloso, and out of which was to grow the city that now bears that name, and later was to give name also to one of the richest counties of the great State of California."

This mission is called after an Italian saint of the thirteenth century, St. Louis, bishop of Toulouse, or to latinize it, "San Luis Obispo de Toloso." St. Louis was born of a noted family, being a grandson of the famous Charles of Anjou, upon whom Pope Urban IV. bestowed the throne of Naples and Sicily. His father, Charles II., married Mary of Hungary, and by her had fourteen children. The eldest of these was Charles Martel, Prince of Salerno, the second was the bishop, Louis, after whom this mission was named; the third, Robert, King of Sicily; the fourth, Philip, Prince of Tarentum. Four sisters married heads of ruling houses, Clementia becoming the wife of Charles of Valois; Bianca married James, King of Aragon; Elenora became wife of Frederick, King of Sicily, and Maria, marrying the King of Majorca.

Luis, once taken prisoner of war, was attacked with a dangerous illness, and vowed that if he recovered he would join the Order of St. Francis. After seven years spent in captivity he was released and immediately proceeded to fulfill his vow. Later he was made bishop of Toulouse, where he made a name for himself even in a day when there were many famous men, and although under 24 years of age when he died. On taking orders he gave up all his great wealth and devoted his few years in the priesthood largely to work among the very poor.

Many of these missions still possess rare old relics of the past. Some of these are quite valuable. Among those of the San Luis is an ancient hand painting, done in Mexico in 1774, by one Jose Paez, and still in a remarkable state of preservation. It is a representation of the baptism of Christ by John the Baptist, and was once used by the early fathers as an altar piece. A crucifix of ancient date and three of the original bells, the latter still in use, are also to be seen at this mission. Many noted characters of past days in California have been at some time connected with the work in this place.

Like all the missions in California, the local station has had its trials and tribulations. In an interesting sketch of this mission, as yet unpublished, Mr. Henry M. Moreno, a native of San Luis Obispo, translates from the original some of the few records still to be found at the mission. He writes as follows: "The early history of

106

the Mission de San Luis Obispo de Tolos is more or less shrouded in mystery and even Father Englehardt, in his 'Franciscans in California,' only devotes a few pages to the events immediately following its foundation. This fact, however, is readily accounted for by the three disastrous fires which occurred within the first ten years of its existence, destroying all records. Father Serra, in his own handwriting, makes a statement in the cover of one of the old, Indian hand-bound books of record (the marriage register), which explains much of the mystery that surrounds the history of this sacred shrine. This explanatory note left by the Father of all Missions in California, states (in Spanish) that in 1776, on the 29th day of November, a conflagration destroyed all the out-buildings on the Mission grounds, except the church and granary, the matrimonial records being consumed in one of the houses which was razed by the fire. This was the work of an unfriendly Indian and the fire was caused by the discharging of burning arrows at the thatched roofs." Such is the simple record of some of the trials and vicissitudes of these missions.

The Mission of San Miguel, dedicated to the Archangel St. Michael, was established on the 25th day of July, 1797. Its founders were Fathers Lausen and Sitjar, two of the most faithful of the early California priests. Like all its companions it too has known days of prosperity and days of adversity. After a number of years during which the services were discontinued, these later were resumed and are regularly conducted at this time.

Churches of the non-Roman obedience were established throughout the county in later days. The City of San Luis Obispo being the oldest established point in the county, and the largest city in this section, it was natural that the churches should find their earliest and largest representation at that point. All the leading denominations are today represented in all the larger towns of the county.

The first of these religious bodies to locate in San Luis Obispo was the Episcopal Church, which was organized in 1867. A few of the members of that communion gathered together in one of the public school buildings, known as the "Mission School," and located on Monterey Street, immediately opposite the original Mission, on August 18th. The meeting was in charge of the Rev. C. M. Hogue, sent to organize the work by Bishop Kip, one of the pioneer clergymen of the coast. The names of many of the men and women of the later period of development of this section are among the number of those present at this meeting or connected a little later with the new organization. The church today is in a very prosperous condition, possessing property located in one of the best residential sections and valued at about $12,000.

The next church to locate in that city was the Methodist, established in 1872 by Rev. M. W. Glover. It now numbers 152 members, and owns property valued at about $20,000. It is well organized and in a prosperous condition. The Presbyterian Church was organized in July, 1874, by the Rev. Mr. Frazer who came down from Oakland, for that purpose. The final organization of this body was affected in May, 1875. Its people now possess a very beautiful building of stone, on one of the most prominent street corners in the city, and is in a very flourishing condition. The Baptist Church was organized in 1892, now has about 75 members, property valued at about $10,000 and has a growing membership. The Christian Church organized in 1910 and the Christian Science Society established in 1913 both have growing memberships, and the German Lutheran Church, established 1908, has since built up a fine property and become one of the most active religious bodies in the community.

San Luis Obispo County has a very heterogeneous population. Its peoples come from all lands and climes. Within a radius of thirty or forty miles of the city proper there reside natives of more than twenty different nations. This affects religious life as it does all the various departments or groupings of the body politic. Probably very few cities in the United States, of its size, possess so mixed a variety of nationalities. There is a veritable "melting pot" of "all sorts and conditions of men," raising many problems of various kinds to be solved by this small section of country.

One result of this gathering of all tongues and nations has been, naturally, a somewhat slow development of the section. On the other hand, the development such as has been made has been of a very substantial character. As time progresses, marked characteristics stand out more and more prominently. If, on some occasions, there is somewhat of indifference manifested towards movements of general community interest that same indifference shows itself at another time in a solidity of purpose that indicates a development in permanent stability; if there be a difference of opinion that sometimes hinders a unanimity of thinking sufficient to prompt aggressive action, that same trait once it is aroused, because it brings to bear a combination of the thought of many men of differing minds, produces a public opinion decisive in action and positive in results. All of these local conditions, while acting at times as a deterrent to positive action of any sort, also indicates that in the general refining process of the community "melting pot" there is slowly being ingrained into the life of the community many strong characteristics such as stand for a very valuable permanent community asset to the future citizenship.

An illustration of this is already noticeable in the religious activity of the community. In times past anything like corporate action among the various Christian bodies was well-nigh impossible. That was nothing peculiar to this particular community, being as is well known a thing common to the religious world irrespective of locality. Today, however, any civic or community problem requiring decisive action can readily summon the united support of different religious bodies. All the ministers of the county as well as leading men and women of the various religious bodies, are today among the ready and willing leaders in all phases of activity that make for community uplift. This is true not alone of matters distinctively religious, but also regarding matters that pertain more strictly to social conditions and general civic or moral welfare. The result is that there is always at hand a weighty influence of the best religious and moral thought of the community ever ready to aid in the religious, social, or civic advance of the people.

In such cordial relations between the pastors of different congregations, and the devotion to Christian ideals of the lay members thereof, lies one of the strong hopes of any community. It is such united effort combined with a conscientious retention of individual ideals, and a tolerance for difference of opinion in others, that is to help solve the great problem of the country church, and thus to bring full pressure to bear upon our rural sections of those spiritual forces that alone can preserve alive the social and civic righteousness of these communities. The decline of the country church is one of the most deplorable facts of the times. This decline probably marks one of the passing phases of the development of our national life, and yet it is one that is of vital import to the future. It is not the place of the writer to go into the cause of this decline, but in writing the history of any section such decline is seen to indicate a condition that cannot be overlooked. It is sufficient for the purpose of this record however, to note that happy condition which today is more or less universal throughout this section, and which indicates a broadening and deepening religious spirit such as manifests itself in a growing tendency towards religious co-operation between various groups of religious affiliations. It speaks well for the future.

And any chronicler of past events in this section must acknowledge that notwithstanding many grave difficulties and a full complement of discouragements, the religious leaders of the past have been men of sterling worth and tried integrity of character. The evidence of the work of these men is amply seen today. Silently and slowly, without any too much encouragement, but with a persistence born of the religious spirit for which they stood, not only priest and minister of the past, but many of the lay folk also, have left their permanent impress upon the times in which they lived and thereby upon the future life of the section. And if they have differed in their ideals, today we note that that really meant to weave a thread of truth into the woof of the community life such as was to have its own peculiar meaning and value not only to the members of their own religious group but also to the social order as a whole.

CHAPTER XIII

CENTRES OF POPULATION

Spreading over so vast an area as 3,334 square miles, the future location at least of many widely separated centres of population was indicated early in the history of the county and from the initial blacksmith shop, store and postoffice, the settlements have grown or stagnated to meet the demands of the surrounding populations. Along the coast line, San Simeon, Cambria, Cayucos, Morro, Avila, Pismo and Oceano were the natural points of vantage as affording more or less favorable access to ocean transportation, their chief if not their only highway to the markets of the world. Shipping facilities were of course primitive. With the exception of Port San Luis Obispo, in a small bight of the bay of that name, there was no sufficient indentation in the coast line to afford protection against the winter storms. The small freighting vessels dropped anchor as closely as they could to the shore and the freight and passengers were handled by boats and lighters or sometimes by derricks that stretched a long arm out over the surf. Wharves were presently erected but many of them were slightly built and in time were swept away to be replaced by better located and more substantial structures. With increasing business, the towns have grown and are adequately supplied with the usual hotels, stores and shops, schools and churches, societies and fraternities. Cambria being some thirty-four miles from the county seat was one of the earliest settlements and controlling the trade and business of the northwest section of the county was for a long time second only to the Mission town in population and importance. It was practically the terminus of the road along the coast. Beyond it stretched far inland from the rocky and precipitous shore line and for many miles in width, an impassable mountain region. It was to skirt this hopeless barrier that Portola went eastward after journeying thus far on his original march of discovery. Here again we can note the far-reaching influence of the great world-war. For through this desolate land a distorted nightmare of gorge and precipice, the State of California, as a measure of defense against a possible invader, has ordered the construction of a military road. It is hardly probable that for any reason less imperative than the safety of the country the road would ever have been built. But being haply deemed essential in time of war it will be highly appreciated in the piping times of peace. It will be a new Camino Real if it should not rather be named the Camino Portola in honor of the great discoverer who was the first to traverse it. It makes continuous, the road following closely the ocean shore from San Francisco to San Luis Obispo and valuable as a new artery for traffic it will afford a wonderfully attractive scenic drive throughout its whole extent. Aside from the business monopoly it enjoyed as the emporium of a great dairy and stockraising country and the supply point for the quicksilver mines in its vicinity, Cambria was fortunate in its beautiful location and surroundings. A striking feature was its forest of pines, found nowhere else in the county, and which from the earliest days and until importation by sea became fairly practicable, supplied the limited amount of timber and lumber used in the county. The rafters in the old Mission which still support its roof are of Cambria pine, shaped by the axes of the Indian workmen. As late as fifty years ago, the timbers and flooring of the Episcopal Church building, erected at that time in San Luis Obispo were made of Cambria pine and still remain intact and unimpaired a tribute to its lasting qualities.

The eastern part of the county awaited the advent of the Southern Pacific Railroad for any urban growth. San Miguel had existed for a century or more but as a Mission only. And when the evil days of the secularization came it practically vanished from the map. Abandonment, decay and intentional destruction did its work and for years only crumbling ruins marked the place which had once been so marvelously prosperous.

Although established twenty-five years after San Luis Obispo had been founded, it had grown to rival the older Mission in importance. It commanded a superior territory. But while the Mission had been practically destroyed and its great holdings had passed into private hands, the advantageous location invited settlement and the town speedily became and has continued to be a flourishing community. Eight miles south lies Paso Robles whose beginnings are pre-historic. Underlying the site of the city are vast deposits of hot mineral water, which in primeval days, boiled to the surface and formed mud springs. Tradition says that the aborigines regarded the mud as an infallible panacea for all the ills that flesh is heir to and came here in multitudes and from great distances to parboil themselves in the mud baths. Their beliefs and practices have survived in the latter day populations but under somewhat different conditions. A half million dollar hotel houses the pilgrims for health and pleasure and the resort is one of the most noted of the kind on the coast. Aside from which the town has great advantages as a business point as is evinced by its steady increase in population. Templeton and Santa Margarita, the next stations on the Southern Pacific Road, were respectively called into being as the terminus for a time during the slow construction of that railroad and each had a couple of years' enjoyment of that distinction during which time enterprising real estate men availed themselves of the opportunity to lay out and sell an extensive array of town lots and secure a ready made population which became permanent and has remained so. South of the county seat, Arroyo Grande, now one of the three incorporated cities of the county, was a spontaneous growth, its marvelous soil and productiveness being compelling factors.

The county seat, from its favorable and central location, due to the prescience of its founder, Padre Serra, has maintained its predominance, politically and financially. It has about one-third of the population and casts about one-third of the votes of the county and the capital and business of the county is concentrated there. Incidentally much has already been said of the early history of the city and while its gradual evolution follows generally that of any other American municipality still the steps of its growth may have interest to the general reader. With the first material accessions of population came the problem of adequate water supply, one not easy of solution. Most cities are favored with adjacent lakes or rivers or artesian sources even in California. That consideration in fact has usually influenced the choice of location. Father Serra was attracted by the abundant water supply, the perennial streams flowing either side of his chosen site and the numerous springs in the vicinity. And the provision which so ample for the needs of the mission proved adequate for it and for the small population which gathered around it for a full century thereafter. For it was only in 1872 the centennial of the Mission, that in American fashion, a franchise was secured to provide water for the town. The demand was limited as yet. Four years before that date, it is of record, the population within the square mile granted to the budding municipality in lieu of the four square leagues to which as an ancient pueblo the city was rightfully entitled, was but 600. But those pioneers of the early '70s were building for the future and with excellent judgment. The census of 1880 showed a population within the township lines of

113

3,754 and water had become the great desideratum. An early achievement of the Mission Fathers was the construction of an acequia or irrigating ditch for the benefit of their orchards and gardens, taking the water from the San Luis Obispo Creek. The later purveyors of water for the growing city have followed their example only extending their effort to meet the increasing demand. The stream meanders down the Cuesta Canyon before traversing the city and gathers its floods from that extensive water shed and the abundant rainfall if it could be stored would supply the wants of a great city. But there are difficulties. The rains sweep down the steep mountain sides, thinly covered with soil or vegetation, swell the streams mightily for a few hours on their rapid flight to the ocean and the natural and artificial reservoirs retain comparatively little of them. So far, however, the storage has been sufficient for the city's necessities. The enterprising citizens who began the task struggled manfully with it for many years but finally transferred their rights and properties to the city for a reasonable consideration. With water supplied, a sewer system became practicable and much agitation therefor ensued. For a time the creek economically served in that capacity, being providentially or diabolically, according to the standpoint of the critic, located with reference to such service. But the creek was not always a roaring flood and when in the rainless months it dwindled to a trickling stream, its incapacity became painfully apparent. The problem was a serious one and engaged the attention of the authorities for years but finally was effectively solved by the adoption of the plans of Col. G. B. Waring. That distinguished engineer, whose great reputation gained in like work in Memphis, Havana, and other large cities, still survives, chanced to be in the state and greatly to the credit of the city fathers of that day they secured his services. Colonel Waring's plans were based upon the exclusion of the storm waters from the sewers. The custom had generally prevailed and is not yet obsolete to use the sewers as conduits for the rains, the washings of the streets and as the general receptacle for rubbish and refuse of all kinds in addition to the sewage proper and to conveniently carry out the idea, easy access to the sewers was provided by innumerable openings, every street corner being supplied therewith and many other places. As sewers rapidly filled up under this system, they had to be of large size and substantial material and required constant and costly labor to keep them serviceable. Waring proposed iron pipes, of capacity limited to the amount of sewage proper they were intended to convey and receiving nothing except from house

114

connections. At convenient intervals along the sewer lines, flush tanks were provided which worked automatically, discharging periodically a calculated volume of water into the pipes, giving a constant added impetus to the flow of sewage to its destination. This ultimate deposit is in septic tanks, aerating beds, etc., located at a lower elevation beyond the town limits. The system seems mechanically perfect and is an abiding monument to the skill and ingenuity of the gifted designer.

Built chiefly of wood and with an always limited water supply, San Luis Obispo, in its earlier days of rapid construction suffered frequently from fires, but, by good fortune chiefly, none were widespread. Energetic and enthusiastic firemen usually succeeded in confining the destruction to the building attacked. Hotels seemed to have been the favorite prey of the flames. The records show seventeen or more destroyed by fire and although most of them were cheaply built, two at least, the Andrews and the Ramona were quite imposing. The frequent fires occasioned much apprehension and enforced strenuous efforts for protection. The citizens have viewed with great satisfaction and relief the progressive steps taken in that direction. But while the city points with pride to its "triple-combination engine and chemical hose auto; its combination chemical engine and hose cart" and other up-to-date paraphernalia, its calm appreciation is not comparable to the enjoyment the town experienced in the acquisition and possession of its first steam fire engine. That was in 1889. Somewhat appalled by the magnitude of the investment (it cost $5,000!), facing more or less opposition, and a probable hole in the treasury, the city fathers bought the machine. It was a "Silsby Rotary," it was proudly claimed, understood to be the finest procurable at the time of its capacity. It was really a powerful machine and proved its worth in many fierce fire fights in the years that followed and is still serviceable. It was quite a dazzling creation, a towering mass of nickel plate, which its obsequious attendants kept polished to the last degree. But the crowning decorative feature was the team of horses purchased for its propulsion. This was a magnificent pair of young Percherons, exactly matched, whose perfection would have delighted the heart of Rosa Bonheur. They were bred in the vicinity from imported stock of the noblest pedigree, wonderfully intelligent, and trained and handled by their driver, a notable horseman, they speedily learned their business and from the first tap of the bell to their volcanic burst from the engine house was a record number of seconds. The fire itself became quite a secondary matter to the crowd that ran to "watch the engine come out" and to see the superb team career along at full gallop, the massive machine swaying and tossing like a toy at their heels, the driver lashed to his seat and the black smoke pouring from the stack. It was the custom of the firemen of that day to have an annual "benefit," a theatrical entertainment, staged by local talent, the play depicting episodes in the lives of the firemen. The star performance, the event of the evening was the advent of the big team, "Frank" and "Rowdy." The horses would come thundering on the stage, dragging their engine and stand at the footlights gazing around at the yelling, uproarious crowded audience as if they quite understood and thoroughly enjoyed the situation. The theatre was well adapted for the event, the stage being nearly level with the ground in the rear. The building had been erected by popular subscription as a pavilion for the holding of agricultural fairs. The stage was large and strongly built and the auditorium was of good dimensions. For many years the pavilion served for all public gatherings, theatrical, political and social. Distinguished politicians spoke from its stage and famous actors appeared there. But nothing had been done to beautify its interior. It was painfully bare and barn-like. Our citizens did not suffer on that account but their pride received quite a jolt when a noted actress who had condescended to visit us, and had not been too well received and who it may be said was more noted for her pulchritude than for her dramatic ability was ungenerous enough to comment derisively on our Thespian temple, on her return to the Eastern states. Perhaps it recalled unpleasantly the early barn-storming period of her career. But the old time-honored structure was after a time fated to abandonment. It was supplanted by a modern building which left nothing to be desired, which was erected by the local lodge of "Elks." San Luis Obispo from its early days was numerously supplied with fraternal organizations. From its isolated position it had to depend for recreation and entertainment upon local effort. Political campaigns brought occasional spell-binders and traveling shows, circuses and theatrical troupes were more common than in these latter days. There was more or less private hospitality but the residences for the most part were not designed for large gatherings and domestic service was a difficult problem. All of which doubtless contributed to the multiplication of lodges and having membership in several of them, the "joiner" was assured of constant opportunity for human companionship. The Odd Fellows were the pioneers but were rapidly followed by Masons of all sorts, Foresters of America and Independent Order of Foresters, Elks, Eagles and Moose, Druids and

116

Red Men, Woodmen and Workmen, Knights Templar, Knights of Pythias and Knights of Columbus, Chosen Friends, Royal Arcanum and Fraternal Brotherhood, U. P. E. C., I. D. E. S. and Dania, Native Sons and Grand Army of the Republic. If there are other orders they were probably present. The wives and daughters of the community exhibited a like interest in lodge gatherings and while some of the lodges included both sexes in its membership the separate organizations of the fair sex were numerous. Among them were the Eastern Star, Rebekahs, Women of Woodcraft, U. P. P. E. C. Native Daughters, Pythian Sisters and Women's Relief Corps besides Civic clubs, Book clubs, Whist clubs and others. All these lodges prospered as a general thing, retained and increased their membership and with a certain frugality laid up some treasure for a day of need. While not unmindful of the avowed charitable and benevolent objects for which they claimed to exist still poverty was rare and opportunity for benevolent assistance infrequent and several of the lodges from their accumulated dues were able to build and own their lodge houses. Among them were the Odd Fellows, Masons, Elks and Knights of Columbus. The lodge of Elks had a material advantage over the others. By the tenets of the order it monopolized the territory half way to Salinas on the north and to Santa Barbara on the south and its membership was drawn from that very considerable area and besides it emphasized the entertainment of its members to a greater degree than other fraternities. The ambition of the lodge grew with its increasing roster and a handsome building was erected only to be torn down in a few years as it became inadequate and upon its site the present structure took its place, a notable one from several points of view. It is a beautiful edifice, chaste and elegant in design and would adorn a location of prominence in a large city. Its lodge room is one of the finest on the coast; its club rooms and various apartments are large and well-appointed and it is richly furnished throughout. But the special pride of the lodge is the theatre which occupies a considerable part of the building. It has a seating capacity of 1,000 and is very correctly planned and finely decorated and equals in all respects theatres of the same size in larger cities. The townsfolk find great satisfaction in it and in the flattering comments of visitors, theatrical and other. But it is the more remarkable as illustrating the lodge spirit referred to. Here is the finest and most costly building in the little town (it cost about $125,000) erected with no prospect or expectation of adequate financial benefit, but merely to gratify the social instincts of the members of the order. In large cities, men

117

of great wealth have luxurious club houses as they have any other accessory of fortune. But the members of a country lodge are not usually overburdened with lucre and by force of circumstances are generally, like Mrs. Gilpin, "of a frugal mind." The Elks' Lodge Building is a monument to the bond of fraternity that delights in labor "for the good of the order" rather than for individual gain. Proportionate to their material strength other lodges, as has been said, have in the same spirit built their homes, adding materially to the improvement of the city, notably the Masonic order which runs a close second to the Elks with a $75,000 investment. Of late years a number of modern business blocks have been erected. The present generation found the city built of wood and, as far as the business section goes will have left it of brick. The public buildings were considerable achievements in their day and are still sufficient for their purposes but have lost their preeminence. The Public Library had quite a struggle for existence and for many years failed to enlist the interest of the general public. A heterogeneous and polyglot population had little use for books and the project waited the coming of a more appreciative class for success. Many were the schemes to create and increase the library fund. Ultimately money enough was accumulated by gift or otherwise to secure at least a permanent home, a twenty year lease of adequate quarters being purchased. Books began to accumulate by purchase and contribution from private collections. Then recourse was had to the good genius of libraries, the philanthropic Mr. Carnegie and by his prompt assistance, a substantial and commodious building was erected, and it being at last recognized by the authorities as a proper object for public support a small tax therefor was included in the annual budget. With the services of a trained librarian and the supervision of a board of directors appointed by the city trustees, the library has become a very popular institution. It has now some 10,000 volumes and a patronage that finds the supply much too limited. The changed attitude of the public in that regard evidences in some degree the change in the population itself, an approach to homogeneity, an effect of the "melting pot," the assimilation to the American pattern and the Californian mould, of its original constituent elements drawn from so many different environments and with such widely varied racial characteristics. Immigration, at least from foreign countries, has greatly diminished in later years and many of those sturdy fortune-seekers, who left their distant birthlands to serve in the building of this newer civilization have passed away. Even for those of them who still remain with us, the days of their youth is a fading memory, to their descendants it is only a tradition. Even to a greater degree than other parts of our country, this section of it is becoming a land of "Native Sons." The new generations are rapidly coming into their inheritance. With but few exceptions, native talent supplies our professional men, doctors, lawyers and judges, fills our offices, civil and political and controls our business communities.

Taken as a whole, considering our urban settlements with reference to their physical conditions and the intelligence and character of their populations, they may be said to have "arrived" and that they compare favorably with any other American communities of like size and environment. The process has been long-continued and gradual. As is obvious from statistics of expenditure and indebtedness of the municipal corporations throughout the country, patient waiting upon the slow processes of Nature fails to satisfy this latter day generation. Time was when only village conditions were demanded or expected in a village even although by virtue of numbers it had attained the dignity of a corporation. But times have changed. Waiting has gone out of fashion. Sleepy, old towns, plodding contentedly on are seized upon by demoniac heralds of progress and are hustled into conformity with the standards of the day. If a new town is projected it must come forth full-panoplied, like Minerva, with no preliminary era of growth vouchsafed. Just as the schoolboy of today begins where Isaac Newton or his latest successor in scientific discovery left off, our latest Californian cities seem to have been set down in their appointed place, ready made, complete in all details and provided with all modern conveniences, a sort of Aladdin's lamp performance. No such magical vision has as yet astonished the natives of this corner of the world but our most recently established centre of population is not without a suggestion at least of the kind. This is the creation of the new Atascadero Colony, a proposition which involves the speedy if not instant transformation, at all events in a practically negligible period of time of a cattle ranch of some thousands of acres into a veritable city, having its municipal centre, miles of perfected avenues traversing its wide area in all directions and on its subdivisions of generous dimensions, beautiful residences, picturesque, individual and particularly modern and up-to-date. Except for the trees and shrubbery, Nature declines to be hurried, there are no beginnings, no intermediate stages. The usual cross-road store, postoffice, blacksmith and butcher shop, vague promises of a possible future, appear only as departments in a great building of steel and reenforced concrete. A massive structure of

119

like magnitude houses what represents the local newspaper where a great force of men and women, with batteries of linotypes and great presses and binderies, all the latest perfected devices in the art preservative, rival the foremost metropolitan publishing houses in the character and multiplicity of the work accomplished and in securing world-wide publicity. The "little red schoolhouse" appears as an edifice of like pretensions, presaging educational facilities of unlimited extent, and in what might be considered the suburban adjuncts to this marvelous community are vast expanses of orchards and cultivated areas and on its further limit on the ocean front easily and quickly accessible are the beaches and surf of the Pacific with all the attractions of a fashionable resort. Commensurate with the ambitions of the founders is the extent of the domain of the community. It comprises over 23,000 acres of land, a princely possession.

Except as a speculative venture, the acquisition of great tracts for future profit, the millionaire class have failed to appreciate this county as a field for investment. In other sections, more particularly the southern part of the state, the gilded globe-trotter provides himself with a gorgeous bungalow for occasional occupancy just as he has a villa on the Riviera or a lodge in the Adirondacks. He is probably not acquainted with his neighbor and does not care to be. His interest in the country is confined to those measures that make for a pleasurable environment, fine roads and beautiful residences. But the descendants of the Argonauts regard these newcomers, climbing over the wall, as accessions of doubtful value. To them, "California" is a people rather than a locality. The new injection is to them something of an infection. As one recent writer, somewhat unkindly but not incorrectly puts it, it is "a transplanted hunk of the Middle West, a mixture of nice old gentlemen and ladies who have worked all their lives and earned the right to play around among the orange blossoms." San Luis Obispo is selfmade; her wealth is of her own creation and her people manifest much content and satisfaction with the work of their hands.

The Biblical worthy whose idea of happiness was that neither poverty nor wealth should be his portion might here share the common lot and find the fruition of his desires. The poor are here, "ye have them always with you" but it is the accident of Nature and not the defeat in a hopeless struggle for existence, and it never goes unaided. If there is no cumbrous wealth there is no want. There are no inclemencies. It is a land of sunshine but the heat is never oppressive, of abundant rains in their season but no winter desolation.

It is the Land of the Happy Medium.

A Timeline of
San Luis Obispo County History
BY
HISTORY IN
SAN LUIS OBISPO
COUNTY
Site by Lynne Landwehr © 2004
www.historyinslocounty.org

1542 Cabrillo and party enter Morro Bay, name Morro Rock (Click here for a timeline of Morro Bay's history, provided courtesy of Jane H. Bailey.)

1769 Portolá expedition passes through the area
1772 Fages leads Spanish expedition to area to secure bear meat for settlements at Monterey and San Antonio
1772 Junípero Serra founds Mission San Luis Obispo de Tolosa, 5th in the coastal chain of 21 missions
1797 Mission San Miguel Arcangel founded (16th mission)

1821-22 California becomes Mexican as Mexico gains independence from Spain
1837-1846 Mexican land grants are made to settlers in area which will become SLO County
1848 Treaty of Guadalupe Hidalgo; California becomes territory of United States
1850 U.S. statehood for California; San Luis Obispo becomes one of California's original 27 counties
1857 Cholame Valley (in SLO County) is epicenter of the historic Fort Tejón earthquake
1858 Vigilante committee formed
1860 County population is 1,782
1862-64 Severe drought kills off most of the cattle on the great ranchos
1864 Portuguese sea captain Joe Clark establishes San Simeon whaling station
1866 Steele brothers commence dairying operations in "cow heaven"
1867 Captain James Cass to Cayucos

1870 County population is 4,772

1873 Construction begins on Harford's Wharf (now Port San Luis) and narrow gauge railway; County Courthouse completed

1874 Ah Louis opens wooden store on Palm Street, City of SLO; Piedras Blancas Lighthouse completed

1875 Developer C. H. Phillips subdivides Rancho Morro y Cayucos into town lots

1878 Beginning of gold rush in the La Panza area

1879 Establishment of County Hospital and Farm

1880 County population is 9,142

1886 Southern Pacific Railroad line arrives in San Miguel, then Paso Robles

1889 El Paso de Robles Hot Springs Hotel replaces early thermal center; Southern Pacific service is extended to Santa Margarita

1890s Quarrying begins at Morro Rock

1890 County population is 16,072; Point San Luis Lighthouse completed

1894 Southern Pacific service is extended to San Luis Obispo, ending stage service over the Cuesta Grade; U.S. requires registration of Chinese residents, who must carry Certificates of Residence or be deported

1900 County population is 16,637

1901 The "gap" in railroad service between SLO and Los Angeles is finally closed; California Polytechnic School founded

1903 California Polytechnic School holds first classes

1906 Union Oil builds first oil pipeline to Avila Beach

1907 Oilport, at site of present Shell Beach, completed in November, then destroyed by heavy surf in December

1910 First flight of an airplane over city of SLO, in a July 4 demonstration

1911 Legal daily limit for Pismo clams set at 200

1913 E.G. Lewis founds Atascadero colony

1922 Construction of Blue Star Memorial Temple in Halcyon

1923 Anderson Hotel opens in city of SLO (July)

1925 Milestone Inn, later known as the Mo-Tel Inn, opens as the country's first "motel"

1926 Union Oil Tank Farm Fire (April 7)

1928 SLO High School built on Murray Hill

1920s-30s: Colony of "Dunites" flourishes in Oceano/Nipomo dunes

1936 W.P.A. begins work on north breakwater, making causeway to

Morro Rock; "Migrant Mother" photographed in Nipomo by Dorothea Lange

1938   Small colony of sea otters spotted in remote area off Big Sur Coast; their recovery will re-extend their range south along SLO coast

1939   Hoover brothers and Art Thompson establish San Luis Obispo airport

1940   County population is 33,246

1941   Camp San Luis is expanded to meet wartime training needs; Union Oil tanker Montebello sunk by Japanese submarine off coast near Cambria (December 23)

1942   U.S. Executive Order 9066 forces relocation of 800 County residents of Japanese ethnicity

1946   First Pismo Beach Clam Festival

1950   County population is 51,417

1958   Hearst Castle opens as state park; Alex and Phyllis Madonna open the Madonna Inn

1960   County population is 81,004

1962   SLO High School building condemned as seismically unsafe; new high school building completed 1963

1965   County population is 102,486

1970s Ongoing protests re licensing of Diablo Canyon Nuclear Power Plant

1985 Las Pilitas fire burns 75,000 acres

1988   FAA control tower added to San Luis Obispo County airport

1990   Elephant seals establish new colony on beach near Piedras Blancas

1990 (August 2) City of San Luis Obispo becomes first place in U.S. to ban smoking in bars.

1993   Chapel Hill at Shandon completed by Judge William P. Clark and his wife Joan Clark

1997   Record grape harvest focuses attention on development of local wine industry

1998   Unocal agrees to $18 million clean-up of oil seepage under Avila Beach

1999   Beginning of Cal Trans project to widen Cuesta Grade portion of Hiway 101

2000   County population is 246,681 (U.S. Census)

2001   Cal Poly celebrates 100th anniversary of its founding

2003 (June) Closure of SLO County General Hospital (est. 1879)

2004 Voters defeat library funding measure and measure to ban modified crops; inroads made by "big box" stores; housing prices continue upwards

Made in the USA
Middletown, DE
07 January 2023

21633037R00080